..and still
The R...
...carry on!

THE BRITISH
HOME FRONT
POCKET-BOOK

1940-1942

Compiled and introduced by Brian Lavery

MINISTRY OF INFORMATION

CONWAY

Compilation and Introduction © Brian Lavery 2010
Volume © Conway 2010

First published in 2010 by Conway,
An imprint of Anova Books Ltd
10 Southcombe Street
London W14 0RA
www.anovabooks.com

Distributed in the U.S. and Canada by
Sterling Publishing Co. Inc.
387 Park Avenue South
New York
NY 10016-8810

10 9 8 7 6 5 4 3 2 1

The image on page 61 reproduced courtesy of the Imperial War Museum
(PST_000057), on page 126 and front endpaper (left) © TfL from the London
Transport Museum collection.

A CIP record for this book is available from the British Library.

ISBN 9781844861224

Printed and bound by WS Bookwell, Finland

Publishers Note.
In this facsimile edition, references to material not included in the selected
extract have been removed to avoid confusion, unless they are an integral part
of a sentence. In these instances, the note [not included here] has been added.

CONTENTS

INTRODUCTION

The history of the Second World War continues to horrify and fascinate us, as can be seen in the school curriculum, in anniversaries and in countless television programmes. The memories of surviving veterans are increasingly cherished, while those of us who were born after the war continue to wonder how we would have done if we had been faced with such a challenge.

The British experience of the twentieth-century world wars is unique. Britain was the only independent nation to fight all the way through both wars without defeat – the dominions of Canada, South Africa, Australia and New Zealand were not independent in foreign policy in 1914. Compared with her European neighbours Britain got of relatively lightly in the Second World War as no part of the homeland (with the rather eccentric exception of the Channel Islands) was occupied by the enemy, and there was no significant land fighting on her soil. Yet the social fabric of the country was completely disrupted by food and clothes rationing, evacuation of children, conscription of both men and women, compulsory direction of labour into certain industries, and devastating air raids. Nearly two hundred years earlier, Dr Johnson wrote that 'Every man thinks meanly of himself for not having been a soldier, or not having been at sea.'[1] Such angst was no longer necessary in 1940, as civilians faced almost equal risks with soldiers, and the nation united – even if the slogan 'Keep calm and carry on' was never actually used at the time. Churchill complained of service personnel in 1944, '… probably not one in four or five men who wear the King's uniform even hear a bullet whistle, or are likely to hear one. The vast majority run no more risk than the civil population of southern England.'[2]

It is highly unlikely we shall ever see an event like the Second World War again. A conflict on that scale between the major nations of the world would be settled by negotiation, unless it led to a rapid and devastating nuclear holocaust. Of course this does not mean that wars have ceased, or that the United Kingdom will never be directly involved in one again – the slow-burning conflict in Northern Ireland lasted for nearly 30 years and caused more than 3,500 deaths from violence.

The documents reproduced here are some of those that were available to the ordinary civilian during the most severe crisis of the war, from 1940 to 1942. They deal entirely with how he or she would have coped with everyday life, independent of any other official activities as an Air Raid Warden, Home Guard member, auxiliary fireman or volunteer worker.

Rationing

Of the basic necessities of life, even good air could not be guaranteed in the early 1940s, and much of British defence planning was based on the premise that the enemy might use poison gases. Everyone was issued with a gas mask, even babies who needed adults to operate the pump to keep them alive. Of course they were never used in practice, but helped to create an atmosphere of fear and of national solidarity, as an emblem of a nation at war.

The second most vital necessity, water, was never a serious problem during the war, except locally when it was feared that bombing might damage the pipes from a reservoir. Food, however, was a constant worry for both the government and the people. After the experience of the First World War, rationing was introduced early in 1940 and gradually extended to cover all kinds of meat, then to more and more kinds of food. It became increasingly important as the U-boat offensive in the Atlantic threatened to cut off imports, but rationing was run very efficiently as different food types were put 'on points' if demand for them was too great.

Wartime cookery books became common as the war went on. Among them was one produced by Elsie and Doris Waters, two singing sisters who adopted the personas of Gert and Daisy, cockney characters whose accents provided relief and amusement among the 'received pronunciation' of Sir John Reith's staid BBC. They broadcast regularly in a programme called 'The Kitchen Front', and this led to *Gert and Daisy's Wartime Cookery Book* in 1941. It had a robust view of working-class life with the slogan of 'feed the brute', and it advised women, 'Don't forget the salt and pepper – you don't want everything to taste like a bit of flannel.' But it was not without patriotism as well as humour

– 'The fish we get in this country is the finest in the world bar none. It's good for you and makes brain. It must do – look at the brains you want to open a tin of sardines.'[3]

Dorothy Cottington Taylor produced a much more upper middle-class version of wartime cookery, as might be expected from the magazine *Country Life*. It had a certain amount of proselytising with chapter headings such as 'The value of milk and cheese' and 'Potatoes are nutritious'. For vegetables it advised, 'It is ... important not only to reduce the cooking but to reduce the quantity of liquid in which they are cooked.' But middle-class housewives had no official privileges when it came to rationing, and careful planning was advised over a fortnight to avoid running out of important ingredients. This is a theme that was taken up by *Ration Dinners* produced by the Central Council for Health Education, which is the first document to be presented in this book. 'A little planning' could 'make the week's rations really last a week' and avoid the problem by which 'so many housewives and canteen managers find that the meat ration is exhausted early in the week'.

The government also provided advice for those running factory canteens, which were vastly expanded during the war and prepared meals in hundreds at a time. This was elaborated on in another wartime pamphlet, *Canteen Catering* issued by the Ministry of Food. It urged canteen managers to introduce unfamiliar food gradually, perhaps into 'dishes which are known and liked, e.g., oatmeal and vegetables into meat pies'. It also had separate recipes 'specially prepared according to Scottish tastes' which were heavy on lentils, black pudding, haggis, herring and Scotch broth. In an emergency when the canteen was disrupted by bombing, the workers could be kept going by stews, hashes and soups.

All the documents on cookery are indicative of the state of the British palate at the time, and in general they were in advance of it in the matter of seasoning and variety. It is doubtful if many of us would find it particularly attractive today.

Clothes rationing was first introduced in May 1941, largely to free many of the 450,000 people employed in the clothing industry for other work. Introducing the scheme, the minister Oliver Lyttelton told the public by radio, 'We must learn as civilians to be seen in clothes that are not so smart, because we are bearing ... yet another share of the war.

When you feel tired of your old clothes remember that by making them do you are contributing some part of an aeroplane, a gun or a tank.'[4] It fitted in with Evelyn Waugh's character Peregrine Crouchback, who 'welcomed the excuse ... to wear his old clothes and to change his linen weekly.'[5] It was almost a patriotic duty to be badly dressed. In occupied countries such as France, it might be regarded as patriotic to look one's best as an act of defiance, while Germany adopted clothes rationing later in the war. All this had much effect on the British reputation for scruffiness, which apparently persists to this day as far away as the White House.

The government adopted the slogan of 'Make do and mend', adapted from the naval practice of having a half-day to 'make and mend' clothes. Ironically this was, in effect, a half-holiday in the navy by 1940, and that was the sense it was used in the radio programme described in the *Radio Times* (see page 135). People were encouraged to repair clothes and to re-use old ones as far as possible.

The *Clothing Coupon Quiz*, which is also included in Chapter 1, was the government's most general attempt to make the public aware of the complex regulations on clothes rationing. It was applied in a wide range of areas, including the armed forces in certain circumstances. Even General Sir Alan Brooke, Chief of Imperial General Staff, was almost caught unawares when a visit to Washington was brought forward and it seemed his warm weather uniform might not be finished on time. 'None of my thin clothes will be ready and all money and coupons will be wasted!!'[6] The *Quiz* includes a list of coupons needed for each item of clothing (not reproduced in this volume), providing a useful guide to the relative values at the time. It gives an eclectic list of items exempted from rationing, from clogs to ballet shoes, from rubber aprons to jockstraps. The rather random order of its Questions and Answers provides some starting juxtapositions – the comic possibilities of trying to buy a single shoe or glove are to be found alongside the answer to the question, 'How are people who have been shipwrecked to obtain clothing?'[7] Clothing is almost a throwaway item nowadays, and the *Quiz* is a reminder how precious it was in 1941, and for some years after the war while rationing continued.

Evacuation

With its deeply entrenched belief that the bombing of cities was likely to be catastrophic from the first days of the war, the government arranged for the evacuation of more than three million children and parents. Most of these returned home when the air raids did not materialise, but many moved out again in the autumn of 1940 as the blitz on London and the other great cities began. Despite many hiccups it was a triumph of planning and organisation, largely achieved by much-maligned government officials and by the voluntary sector. At the centre was the Women's Voluntary Service (which had not yet had 'Royal' added to its title). It had been founded in 1938 partly as an alternative to the Women's Institute, whose pacifist origins prevented it taking a full part in the war effort. The WVS had more than 300,000 volunteers by the start of the war and produced numerous leaflets on evacuation, civil defence and other social issues.

Despite severe paper rationing, some aspects of the war inspired a great deal of publishing, including cookery and air raids. The Home Guard was particularly popular in this respect and at least 130 books with Home Guard in the title were published before the force was disbanded in 1944. These included manuals, magazines, cartoons, plays, novels and even a children's book. They were written from every conceivable point of view, from retired brigadiers of very conservative opinions to former communists who had fought in the Spanish Civil War. This was far less true of evacuation. A handbook telling city mothers and children how to cope with life in the country, or one which told county matrons how to deal with evacuated children with very different attitudes and standards, would have been an invaluable social document. Certainly there was a substantial amount of literature issued within the organisations involved in evacuation – local authorities, railway companies, schools, voluntary organisations and many others. There were many social studies of evacuation, often conducted during or very soon after the event, and it featured strongly in fiction even as it was happening – for example in Evelyn Waugh's *Put Out More Flags* of 1943 and the film *Went the Day Well* (1943). It continues to fascinate, as in, for example, the novel *Goodnight Mister*

Tom published by Michelle Magorian in 1981, and filmed starring John Thaw in 1998; and the children's 'reality' television series *Evacuation* of 2006–08.

But unfortunately no one did much at the time to offer detailed advice to either evacuees or their hosts. Perhaps the experience was too new and unpredictable for people, perhaps it was a social minefield in which class divisions that were supposed to have been narrowed by the war would have been opened up again. The advice of country ladies on how to deal with the disruptiveness and uncleanliness that they expected from the people of the East End of London or the slums of Liverpool and Glasgow would not have looked well in print; nor would the complaints about snobbery and patronising attitudes that the evacuated adults might have written about.

Instead, the evacuees and hosts were left with some rather basic leaflets. In *Evacuation, Why and How?*, reproduced in Chapter 2, the government went to some trouble to explain it to a doubtful public a month before the war started. It also listed the 'evacuable' areas, including most of the industrial towns and cities as far north as central Scotland – though not in the southwest of England, because at that time there was no reason to expect the enemy would occupy France. Other leaflets followed early in 1940 once the initial scheme had apparently failed and people had returned in large numbers. At that moment the government assured the public that 'Evacuation will not be ordered until air raids have taken place or it is clear they are going to begin', but it continued to encourage voluntary evacuation. Meanwhile the National Safety First Association issued its leaflet on *Safety Hints for the Town Child in the Country*. In fact the title was misleading, a large part of it was devoted to items such as safety on the roads, in which the only specifically rural piece of advice was to face the oncoming traffic where there was no footpath. The section 'In the house' was perhaps more concerned with children left unattended than with any particular problems in country cottages. *War Time Play Schemes for Children* is also rather vague about detail, while *Notes and Suggestions on Clothing* tends to assume a high level of ignorance on the art of its readers – '... children will need warmer and harder-wearing clothes and stronger footwear than at home, because they will be walking on wet and muddy roads and running about among trees and bushes.' The latter two leaflets are also in Chapter 2.

In addition, the WVS had leaflets on *Information on Evacuation for Householders Taking Unaccompanied Children* (nd), *General Information on Evacuation for Reception Areas* (nd), *Information for Householders Taking Evacuees* (1944), *Information on Bed-Wetting for Householders Taking Unaccompanied Children* (1944), and *The Cleansing and Care of Children's Heads* (nd).[8]

Conscription

Of course not everyone had the choice of remaining a civilian in wartime. Conscription had been the subject of fierce debate in Britain at the beginning of the century, and was only introduced in the middle of the First World War. By 1939 it was accepted that the only fair way to raise mass armed forces and find workers for industry at the same time was by some form of compulsion. It was first applied in June 1939, when men were called up for six months' training. This was quickly overtaken when the war started and the National Service (Armed Forces) Act was passed, making all men between the ages of 18 and 41 liable for service for an indefinite period. After that, men were called out to register by age group as required. Conscription for women was introduced by a further act of 1941, and the age for men was extended to 51. Many people were exempted from service, including those considered essential to war work, whose occupations were listed in 107 pages of the *Schedule of Reserved Occupations*.

For a mainstream view of the law and how it applied to individuals, a citizen might turn to Robert Pollard's 48-page pamphlet *You and the Call-Up, a Guide for Men and Women.* This gave 'a summary of the powers of the government and other bodies to conscript people, to prevent them from changing their jobs, and to impose restrictions in connection with employment.'[9] For an alternative view of conscription and of society as a whole, he might look at Guy Aldred's pamphlet on conscientious objection in Chapter 3.

Aldred was born in London in 1886 but moved to Glasgow at the time of the First World War, during the period of 'Red Clydeside'. He was imprisoned several times as a conscientious objector and after the war he refused to support either the new Communist Party or the parliamentary aims of the Labour Party. He was not opposed to violence as such and supported the anarchist cause in the Spanish Civil War from 1936–39, but he questioned the state's right to force men to fight for it in any form. His resistance to conscription was absolute and uncompromising, but he did not advise resisters to get out of it by faking illness or citing aged or sick relatives; instead he urged them to fight their cases all the way through the tribunal.

Britain had quite liberal laws on conscientious objection, though not nearly liberal enough for Aldred. At first many did not believe that the Chamberlain government was serious about fighting the Nazis, and in April George Orwell wrote: 'Except for small sections such as Pacifists etc. people want to get it settled & I fancy they'd be willing to go on fighting for 10 years if they thought the sacrifices were falling equally on everybody, which alas isn't likely with the present government in office.'[10] But when an all-party coalition took office as the German attack on Western Europe began in May 1940, the socialist J. P. W. Mallalieu had a change of heart: 'when Churchill formed a National Government with the full support of the Labour Party and when Germany smashed through Belgium, Holland and France and what remained of the British army escaped through Dunkirk; my own previous attitude to the war seemed irrelevant and possibly wrong-headed. I had registered as a Conscientious Objector, on political, not pacifist grounds; and I now withdrew this registration and awaited call-up.'[11] The numbers of conscientious objectors fell constantly with each registration during the crisis of 1940, from more than 5,800 in March to less than 2,000 in July and August.

Air Raids

Like the Home Guard, air raids inspired a very extensive literature at the time. It began some time before the war, because there was a greatly exaggerated belief in the dangers of air raids. Based on some rather spurious studies of the First World War, the RAF believed that there were likely to be fifty casualties for every ton of bombs dropped –

SEPTEMBER 3rd 1939   SEPTEMBER 3rd 1940

THE SIREN! LOOK OUT!

it was estimated that 600,000 people would be killed and twice as many injured in the first sixty days of bombardment. And there was no hope of preventing this by fighter aircraft – in 1932 the Prime Minster, Stanley Baldwin, had stated that 'the bomber will always get through' and that was still the common belief in 1939, even if radar was being developed secretly to help the defence.

In fact the bombing was not nearly as bad as feared. Destruction of cities was only the secondary aim of the Luftwaffe, after support of the army, and it never had the heavy bombers that were necessary for an effective campaign. Day bombing was found to be impossible within days of the start of the war, as the RAF suffered heavy losses over Germany, and found it very difficult to get anywhere near the target. And even when bombs were dropped on London from September 1940 onwards, they killed an average of less than 1.5 people per ton. Total casualties in the major blitz of 1940–41 totalled around 40,000 killed – tragic enough for those involved and shocking to modern sensibilities, but far less than expected. As Churchill wrote of the air force staff in 1941, 'Before the war we were greatly misled by the pictures they painted of the destruction that would be wrought by air raids. This is illustrated by the fact that 750,000 beds were provided for air-raid casualties, never more than 6,000 being required.'[12]

Apart from being evacuated to the country, the city dweller had several alternatives for sheltering during air raids, largely depending on what type of house or flat he lived in. Those in flats were unlikely to make them safe, and were reliant on communal shelters, which might include specially constructed structures, or the impromptu protection of the London Underground system. People with adequate gardens or open space might build their own shelters, most commonly the Anderson Shelter which mainly used earth and corrugated iron. Internally, a house which was otherwise safe could use a Morrison Shelter, a rectangular steel construction whose functional ugliness could be concealed by doubling it up as a table.

Chapter 4 opens with *Your Home as an Air Raid Shelter*, which was produced in the spring of 1940, before serious raids started, and offered another alternative – to make a substantial home as bomb-proof as possible. This had the great advantage that it was not necessary to leave the house to go into a cold, damp and often flooded shelter. The pamphlet was generally optimistic in an age of gloom. The 'zone of destruction' of a bomb was quite small. 'In fact houses offer a great deal of protection against blast and splinters – as well as aerial machine gun fire and splinters of the anti-aircraft shell, the dangers of which you must not underrate – and they can easily be made to afford much more.' Even dwellers in upstairs flats were offered some comfort, provided they could reach an arrangement with their neighbours downstairs, or use a communal entrance hall – a practice which was quite common in Scottish tenements, for example. The key to the protection was a 'refuge room' preferably on the ground floor or basement and with as few windows and openings as possible. The pamphlet assumed that the householder would do most of the conversion himself, though it did not exclude the possibility of employing a builder. Along with the self-assembly Anderson and Morrison shelters, all this tended towards another post-war British characteristic for do-it-yourself home improvements. The booklet concluded with some very practical advice on what to do if caught in the open during an air raid.

The *A.R.P. at Home: Hints for Housewives* went into more advice about keeping shelters clean and tidy and appropriate behaviour while in a communal shelter as well as matter-of-fact information on dealing with incendiary bombs and fitting gas masks. A sizeable extract from it has been reproduced, omitting sections on Being a Good Neighbour, Pets and First Aid.

After the Raid was produced by the Ministry of Home Security in December 1940, and unlike *Your Home as an Air Raid Shelter* it was based on real experience. It begins by acknowledging that civilian victims of raids have been 'in the front line'. But after that it is surprisingly blunt to a modern reader, with little recognition of what the victim must have suffered with the loss of possessions, perhaps a near-death experience, and possibly the loss of close friends and relatives. In a sense the leaflet comes as close as anything actually issued to the spirit of 'Keep calm and carry on', though almost to the point of callousness.

One of the best-known slogans of the war was 'Is your journey really necessary', originally intended for civil servants but soon applied to the general public by means of posters at railway stations. Travel by private car over long distances was almost impossible due to fuel rationing, while the evacuation of children, the movement of troops, bomb damage, air raid delays, shortage of labour and many other factors made rail travel extremely slow and uncomfortable. There were plenty of stories of long hours in packed corridors and compartments with no access to food or water, and of children being passed over the heads of adults to go to the toilet.

As well as its usual function in getting Londoners to and from work, and to shopping and entertainment to a reduced extent, the Underground system provided shelter to millions from the Luftwaffe's raids. At first the authorities resisted the public's desire to take refuge in the Underground, fearing that a 'deep shelter' mentality would lead to defeatism. But it was impossible to stop people buying platform tickets and staying for the night, and by 1 October 1940 when London Transport issued its first notice on *Shelter in Underground Stations* there was a grudging acceptance of the practice, provided regular passengers were able to have access to the trains. This had been refined within the week, when definite hours were set for the use as a shelter, and the idea of a white line 4 feet from the edge to allow room for passengers.

Naturally citizens found ways to amuse themselves during the long nights, and a few of them tried to produce newssheets. *The Swiss Cottager* (a name which sounded perfectly innocent at the time) was intended for the shelterers in the Underground station of that name, just to the north of Regents Park and on the area between inner London and the suburbs. By its fourth issue it seems to have descended into a diatribe against the medical authorities who had failed to set up adequate facilities at the station. *The Subway Companion*, first issued in December 1940, had broader aims and was intended for the whole network. The first issue provided a potted history of life in the tunnels so far.

> . . . things were at first imperfect, many of us spent innumerable hours each day to get a place for our families on platforms. Quarrels and arguments developed, breeding suspicion and ill-feeling. The passengers too were annoyed, their transport had to go on. Out of confusion, however, order slowly began to emerge. Came the White Line system. 4.00 and 7.30 p.m., London Transport insisted we bought tickets and you couldn't blame them. But it was not yet perfect. The Government being alarmed at the enormous number of people sleeping communally, began to make investigations

Two diagrams from the pamphlet *How to put up your Morrison "Table" Shelter.*

into the Tube and other shelterers' problems. Were there possibilities of illnesses in the future? Could shelterers be supplied with food? Officialdom was now in working, but things began to make headway. First Aid Posts were set up at each station. Sanitary conditions were being improved, and at several stations canteens were installed. Then came the Marshal System and the registering of our names for a regular place each night. Some co-operation was becoming evident between Station Staffs and Shelterers, – and our 'Subway Homes' began to take on a new aspect.

The *Companion*'s editor, S. P. Harris, was immensely proud that copies were accepted by the British Museum (later the British Library) where they can be seen to this day. One would like to be more confident in the editorial skills of the team, but by the second issue of January 1941 they were relying rather too heavily on very weak jokes. However, they do give a few insights into the concerns of those in the shelters, such as the concerts staged for Christmas and the existence of the All London

LONDON SLEEPS

Tube Shelter Committee. In fact only two issues of the *Companion* were received by the British Museum, and there is no sign that it carried on beyond that. The role of Underground stations as air-raid shelters has entered the folk memory of London, and one of the most shocking things about the bombings of 7 July 2005 was that three of them took place in the Underground, turning a place of safety to one of danger.

The word 'queue' entered the language from the French and originally meant the tail of an animal. By the eighteenth century it meant a pigtail, as worn by soldiers and sailors at the time. It is first noted in its modern meaning – as a line of people – in 1837 at the time of Queen Victoria's coronation as well as the early part of the railway age – for station ticket offices were often the places where the earliest queues formed. The British are often considered to be obsessed with queuing, and this reputation was greatly boosted during the Second World War. People might have to queue for entertainment, such as dance halls or cinemas, or for more vital matters, such as foodstuffs – there were no supermarkets in those days, and a housewife might have to stand for several hours a day at the butcher's, grocer's, greengrocer's and so on, perhaps to find that supplies had run out by the time she reached the front. Public transport was grossly overcrowded, so queuing for buses and trains was especially important – a serviceman might find himself on a charge if he did not get back in time from his precious leave. The situation was further disrupted by the presence of numerous refugees and foreign nationals who did not necessarily understand the British custom. This was what caused the Ministry of War Transport to issue Statutory Rule and Order No. 517 in March 1942 – 'A person shall not take or endeavour to take any position in a queue or line ... otherwise than behind the persons already forming the same...' It did not state what the penalties were for infringing this rule, other than the obvious hatred of those already in the queue. The Statutory Rule and Order is faithfully reproduced on page 154.

Radio & Cinema

Radio (usually known as 'wireless' at the time) and cinema were by far the most important media of the time. Television was very rare before the war and was suspended during it, while newspapers lacked the immediacy of radio and the dynamism of cinema. Everybody remembered Neville Chamberlain's mournful radio announcement of the beginning of the war and thrilled to Churchill's rousing speeches. Many also listened to enemy broadcasts, especially those from William Joyce or 'Lord Haw-Haw' in Berlin, as an alternative to official information. The BBC only had two stations at the time, the Home Service which eventually became Radio 4 and the Forces Programme which was not just aimed at members of the armed services and eventually became the Light Programme and then Radio 2. Among its programmes on 24 February 1942 (see page 135) was no. 10 in the series 'Make and Mend', aimed at naval listeners. It included a 'yarn' spun by Esmond Knight, the actor who had lost his sight during the battle with the *Bismarck* in 1941, a comic letter to Mrs Wilson from her son Stoker 'Tug' Wilson, the comedy adventures of 'two simple sailors', 'The Briny Trust' a naval version of the famous 'Brains Trust', including a cadet rating under training as an officer and Roland Blackburn and Robert Burgess, two ratings who published a book on naval customs in 1943.[13] Other programmes included, almost incredibly, the snooker champion Joe Davis with hints 'for the average player'.

Radio could be used for highly practical purposes such as calling out groups of reservists at the start of a war. It was primarily a medium of entertainment and education, and the BBC was determined not to become a pure government propaganda machine. But there was still plenty of scope for getting a message across, in the form of practical announcements of new rationing regulations or calling out new classes of men for conscription, to the majesty and grandeur of Churchill's famous broadcasts to the nation and the world.

General Sir Hugh Elles's broadcast of 5 June 1940, in Chapter 5, falls somewhere between these two. It was only two days since the evacuation of Dunkirk had been completed, the war in the rest of France was still going on as Churchill tried to persuade the French Government not to surrender, but already the British were beginning to feel that the Germans would not stop at the English Channel. Elles pointed out that the same danger had been faced against Napoleon in 1805, and to a lesser extent during the 1914–18 war. He urged alertness and responsibility among the civilian population, and urged people to move away from the coast if they could. He ended with the injunction, 'And in the meantime – Carry right on!'

Film is often more difficult than radio to use as propaganda. Unlike radio or television it is not beamed into the home, and one has to make a certain amount of effort to go to a cinema. Even the most totalitarian regime is not likely to force people to go. Both the Soviet Union and Nazi German failed notably in the use of film as propaganda, with the notable exception of the works of Sergei Eisenstein and Leni Reifenstahl – whose works were in any case far more popular with the critics than the masses. In Britain, as elsewhere, the cinema was mainly a means of escaping the drudgery of the war. As Churchill wrote of his own tastes, 'The cinema is a wonderful form of entertainment and takes the mind away from other things.' It was highly popular and 32 per cent of the population went at least once a week, while 38 per cent more went occasionally. They did not go to see war propaganda, the great bulk of films shown were American and escapist, including musicals, westerns, romances and gangster films. Perhaps the most successful attempt to combine propaganda with comedy was Charlie Chaplin's *The Great Dictator*, which was the first from Hollywood to risk the German market by attacking the Nazis, and satirised the German leader. Actual war films had a hesitant start after 1939. Productions such as *Convoy* and *Ships with Wings* offered rather unrealistic views of warfare in which romance was at least as important as action. They were slated by the critics, though quite popular with the public. British war films only got into their stride with Noel Coward's *In Which We Serve* in 1943. In the meantime Hollywood produced *Mrs Miniver*, offering a rather romantic view of the home front and the British class system.

However, the cinema did offer more direct opportunities for information and propaganda in the form of the short films which were part of every evening's entertainment. Even this was not infallible, some cinema-goers deliberately arrived after the start of the programme to avoid them. (In Germany in 1942, as the war news became much worse, groups of people gathered outside cinemas waiting for the newsreels to end, until the government decreed that no one was to be allowed in after the start of the programme.[14]) Once in, if the films were too unsubtle they might attract the jeers of a British audience.

The film documentary movement was strong in Britain before the war under the leadership of John Grierson, and it carried a message of social reform. It was only natural that it should be co-opted into the war effort by the Churchill government, though Grierson himself went off to work in Canada. *Britain at Bay*, also presented in Chapter 5, was one of the first fruits of the work of the General Post Office Film Unit, which became the Crown Film Unit at the beginning of 1941. It used the voice of J. B. Priestley, whose 'Postscript' broadcasts at the height of the crisis of 1940 were as popular as Churchill's, and who was taken off the air because of his left-wing views. But none of this was reflected in *Britain at Bay*, which quoted Churchill's 'fight on the beaches' speech, and emphasised national unity rather than political divisions. It was also in denial about the British Empire – 'these people of ours – as easy-going and good natured as any folk in the world – who asked for nothing belonging to others but only fair dealing among nations . . .'. *Britain at Bay* was produced mainly for home consumption, though a version known as *Britain on Guard* was shown overseas. The unit went on to produce more morale-boosting films such as *London Can Take It* and *Christmas Under Fire*, as well as longer works such as *Target for Tonight* on the RAF and *Close Quarters* on submarines.[15]

Work

There was another great migration during the war years, though it was carried out at a much slower pace and had less emotional impact than the evacuation of children. Skilled men in vital industries were exempt from conscription, but there were far too few of them in the key sectors such as munitions and aircraft, partly because the great depression of the 1930s had led to a lack of apprenticeships, and partly because of an enormous expansion by the use of 'shadow factories'. The gap was largely filled by women. Before the war it had been rare for married women to work unless the family was short of money. During the war, and especially after the factories got into their stride by 1941, it was considered normal and women, mostly unmarried, were also conscripted for factory labour. It is not quite true to say that British women were mobilised to a greater extent that other countries – Germany already had a high level of female employment, largely in small farming, before the war;[16] but Britain lacked Germany's supplies of forced labour and used conscription more widely than others. The position of wartime women workers was highlighted in the feature film *Millions Like Us* of 1943, which was quite successful both as propaganda and as a cinematic experience. It was preceded by short films from the Ministry of Information, including *Transfer of Skill* of 1940 and *Night Shift* in 1942.

In Chapter 6, *On Your Way to the New Job* gives a rather rosy picture of industrial life, with paternalistic foremen, excellent medical services and no sign of conflict between management and workers. It assumes a very low level of knowledge in the new worker: 'Machines are very obedient things, but they will usually only stop when someone makes them stop, so be sure in the first place that you know how to do this.' *Welcome to the War Worker* was aimed at the potential landlord, who was usually assumed to be 'the head of the household'. It gives a few hints at the social conditions of the time. It was not taken for granted that a house, even one large enough to take in at least one lodger, had a bath. The tenant who was *Going Away on War Work*, on the other hand, was assumed to be dealing with the landlady, who would provide meals and call in the district nurse if the tenant became ill.

Invasion

Of course an invasion of the country would have been the greatest test, when the slogan 'Keep calm and carry on' really would have been used. It seemed a strong possibility after the German army swept through The Netherlands, Belgium and France in the spring and summer of 1940 – their air force was strong, their army seemed unbeatable on land, and the capture of Norway that spring seemed to show that they could command the sea as well. Churchill himself was often sceptical about the chance of invasion. In June 1940 he told the House of Commons, '…it seems to me that as far as seaborne invasion on a great scale is concerned, we are far more capable of meeting it today than we were at many points in the last war and during the early months of this war …'. More privately he told his staff that he hoped 'to drown the bulk of them in the salt sea'. But the threat was very useful in building up civilian involvement in the war, and he also told his staff, 'the great invasion scare … is serving a most useful purpose: it is well on the way to providing us with the finest offensive army we have ever possessed and it is keeping every man and woman tuned to a high pitch of readiness. He does not wish the scare to abate therefore, and though personally he doubts whether invasion is a serious menace he intends to give that impression, and to talk about long and dangerous vigils, etc., when he broadcasts on Sunday.'[17] But this view was not shared by the generals, and it was not the one put across to the general public, who joined the Home Guard in huge numbers in the summer of 1940.

The advice issued was no doubt sincere enough. The general public was of course essential to the war effort in many ways, but in the event of an actual landing it was more likely to be a nuisance. Strategists were well aware of how columns of refugees had clogged up the roads in France and made counter-attack even more difficult. They were equally aware of the terror that had been spread among the refugees by dive-bombing and machine-gunning, and were determined to prevent it. A scheme to evacuate all the seaside towns in the likely invasion areas was drawn up. It was never enforced compulsorily, but people were encouraged to move out and many did. As for the rest of the country, the government was firm in its instructions for civilians to 'stay put' once the enemy was in the area, as outlined in Chapter 7. There was no point in fleeing in any case. 'If you do not stay put you will stand a very good chance of being killed.' As to more general advice, the government instructions were to disable any kind of vehicle, to avoid spreading rumours, and to do nothing that might help the enemy in any way.

With hindsight and access to the enemy records it seems that Churchill was right, that invasion was never really likely. It is not quite clear whether Hitler intended it as a bluff or not, but as a classic opportunist he probably never knew that himself. His army was exhausted after its unexpected success against France, his navy was weak after losses of destroyers in Norway, and he had no landing craft which could place large numbers of tanks on British beaches. But the British people did not known that in the summer and autumn of 1940 as they watched the RAF fighting the Battle of Britain over their heads, and made their plans on what to do when, rather than if, the enemy landed.

Conclusion

A conflict of the scale of the Second World War is not likely to happen again but we cannot ignore the possibility of nuclear attack, terrorism, pandemic, financial collapse and environmental disaster. We should look to the wisdom (and occasionally the folly) of our recent ancestors to see how they coped with disruption and danger. As with all wars, the threats they dealt with were not quite the ones that had been planned for, and everyone needed a great deal of resourcefulness and flexibility to survive. That in itself might be a lesson for the future.

As well as giving us some ideas about how the people coped with these extraordinary years, the documents tell us much about how the British character was formed. Bland and monotonous food, scruffy dressing and an obsession with queuing were all well known in Britain before the war, but were greatly reinforced by it, especially since rationing continued for some years afterwards and the attitudes of a whole generation were shaped by it. It has been suggested that queuing is less strictly observed than in the past, and certainly it is far rarer in London to see an orderly bus queue as demanded by the Ministry of War Transport in 1942. That is perhaps a matter of regret, but hardly anyone will deplore the much greater variety and quality of food that has become available in Britain over the last fifty years or so.

[5] Evelyn Waugh, *Sword of Honour*, London, 1984, p.483

[6] Lord Alanbrooke, *War Diaries*, London, 2001, p.265

[7] Questions 71 and 73

[8] The Women's Royal Voluntary Service archives are closed until 2012, so it has not been possible to look at these in detail

[9] London, 1942, p.4

[10] Orwell, *Collected Essays, op cit*, Vol. 1, pp.528-29

[11] J. P. W. Mallalieu, *On Larkhill*, London, 1983, p.198

[12] Martin Gilbert, *The Churchill War Papers*, 1941, London, 2000, p.1313

[13] Robert Blackburn and Roland Burgess, *We Joined the Navy*, London, 1943

[14] Susan Techel, *Nazis and the Cinema*, London, 2007, p.193

[15] BFI, *The British Documentary Movement* 1930-1950, pp.24-32

[16] Adam Tooze, *The Wages of Destruction*, London 2006, pp.358-9

[17] Martin Gilbert, *The Churchill War Papers*, 1940, London, 1994, *op cit*, Vol. II, pp.363, 478, 511

CHAPTER 1

RATIONING

RATION DINNERS
*Homely Savoury Dishes adapted to war
conditions for Families & Canteens*

The Central Council for Health Education
Tavistock House, Tavistock Square, London, WC1

April 1941

FAMILY RATIONS *per week*		CANTEEN RATIONS *per week*	
Meat, per head	1/-	Meat, per 7 meals service	1/-
Fat,* per head........................	½ lb.	Fat,* per meal service	$^1/_6$ oz.
Sugar, per head	½ lb.	Sugar, per meal service	$^1/_{10}$ oz.

*Excluding dripping and suet

MEAT FOR 14 DAYS FOR FOUR ADULTS			MEAT FOR 14 DAYS FOR 100 IN CANTEENS
First week			**First week**
1 lb. minced meat at 10d.	per	lb.	25 lbs. minced meat (any fresh meat)
2 lbs. shoulder lamb at ½	„	„	38 lbs. shoulder and leg of mutton
½ lb. beef pieces at 1/-	„	„	12 lbs. beef pieces
½ lb. breast mutton at 8d.	„	„	12½ lbs. breast mutton
Second week			**Second week**
1 lb. minced meat at 10d.	per	lb.	25 lbs. minced meat
2 lbs. roasting beef at ½	„	„	36 lbs. beef for roasting
½ lb. breast mutton at 8d.	„	„	12½ lbs. breast mutton
½ lb. beef pieces at 1/-	„	„	12½ lbs. beef pieces
			2 lbs. ox liver

⅓ pint bottle of milk should be taken with each of the school meals in order that they may provide rather more than ⅓ of the total calories required daily and a reasonable amount of first-class protein.

The family of 4 adults works a garden. The vegetables are home-grown; jam, pickles, bottled fruit and tomatoes are processed at home.

Foreword

A little planning can make the week's rations really last for a week, and this book sets out to give you just such a simple ground-plan, on which you can build a fortnight's catering, either for the family or the canteen, with the rations allocated to you.

The meat ration is planned to supply savoury dishes for thirteen out of the fourteen days. Fat and sugar are 'spread-out' by the occasional serving of soup or a salad as one of the two courses instead of a sweet.

Should the full meat ration be not available, or not available in the form specified, other nourishing meals are suggested to fill in any gaps. It should, however, be emphasized that no diet is complete without vegetables. Each day's meals should include two helpings of vegetables, one of which should be a salad.

In cooking vegetables, as little water as possible should be used, in order to preserve their vitamins and mineral salt content; also it must be stressed that bread eaten with or between meals should, if possible, be National Wheatmeal. This is now on sale in most shops, and the cost is the same as that of ordinary white bread.

As so many housewives and canteen managers find that the meat ration is exhausted early in the week, and complain that the fat and sugar rations 'will not go round', this little book, with its carefully planned, simple and traditional meals, adapted to war conditions, will serve a useful purpose and show countless women how to get the very utmost out of their rations.

Fresh meat mince, with greens, potatoes, and baked suet pudding; with apple or dried fruit and custard

FOR THE FAMILY (4)
FRESH MEAT MINCE

½ lb. minced meat (raw)   1 teaspoonful salt   1 oz. dripping
¼ teaspoonful pepper   1 onion or meat flavouring essence   1 oz. flour or
fine oatmeal   gravy colouring   ½ pint water   4 ozs. rice, if liked

1. Melt the dripping and fry the onions until savoury. Stir in the mince. Heat together for a few minutes.
2. Pour in most of the water and seasoning and cook gently for 1 hour.
3. Blend the flour with remaining water, add to the mince and cook for a further 10 minutes. Add 1 teaspoonful of parsley; serve with toast or hard baked bread. While the mince is cooking, wash the rice and boil it in fast boiling water for about 15 minutes until tender. Strain it, wash it, and dry in a cool oven on the dish on which the mince is to be served, covered with another plate.

FOR THE CANTEEN (100)

12½ lbs. raw minced meat   2 lbs. onions, if possible   4 ozs. dripping
1½ gallons water   1¾ lbs. fine oatmeal or 1½ lbs. flour   2 ozs. salt and
¼ oz. pepper   gravy browning   parsley   52 lbs. potatoes   30–40 lbs. greens
12½ lbs. wholemeal bread

Season sufficiently and carefully

Roast lamb, sprouts, potatoes steamed in jackets; jam and, or currants in, pastry

FOR THE FAMILY (4)

Half shoulder of lamb

Cut a ribbon of peel from each potato
[No British woman needs instruction on how to roast meat]

FOR THE CANTEEN (100)

38 lbs. leg and shoulder of mutton, boned   1 lb. dripping
For gravy: 2 gallons water from vegetable boiling, as far as possible, and 1 lb. flour and
fine oatmeal mixed   52 lbs. potatoes   25 lbs. sprouts   12½ lbs. bread

Careful seasoning

Cold roast lamb, baked potatoes, vegetable salad, red cabbage pickle; bread and butter pudding

FOR THE FAMILY (4)
VEGETABLE SALAD

1 large cooked beetroot   1 carrot, raw and grated   1 large potato, cut in cubes
2 sprouts, shredded very finely   watercress or lettuce   pepper, salt, a little vinegar,
nut oil and sugar

Cut neatly and arrange attractively. Sprinkle with pepper,
salt, vinegar, sugar and oil.

FOR THE CANTEEN (100)

12 lbs. potatoes, cooked   8 lbs. beetroot, cooked   6 lbs. carrots, grated
1 lb. sprouts or cabbage heart, shredded   1 lb. onions, minced   42 lbs. potatoes
12½ lbs. bread   pepper, salt, vinegar and oil

Braised steak or rabbit, baked potatoes, leeks or mashed parsnip; stewed apple and cornflour

FOR THE FAMILY (4)
BRAISED STEAK OR RABBIT

½ lb. stewing steak (or a rabbit)   ½ oz. dripping   onion   3 carrots, cut into large dice
1 oz. flour   ¾ pint water or vegetable liquor   seasoning and 1 teaspoonful vinegar
gravy colouring
For dumplings: 2 ozs. grated potato, 3 ozs. self-raising flour, 2 ozs. suet

1. Cut the steak or rabbit into eight pieces.

2. Fry the sliced onion and after a few minutes fry the pieces of steak.
3. Sift in the flour and stir.
4. Add the water. Bring to boil, season and put in carrots.
5. Put the pan in the oven or turn into a casserole and bake for 2 hours.
6. Add dumplings ½ hour before the stew is cooked.

FOR THE CANTEEN (100)

12½ lbs. meat without bone   1½ lbs. flour or 1¾ lbs. fine oatmeal   4 ozs. dripping
1 lb. onions   12 lbs. carrots   2 gallons water, or vegetable liquor
1 tablespoonful vinegar   2 tablespoonfuls salt   1 teaspoonful pepper   52 lbs. potatoes
30 lbs. parsnips   12½ lbs. bread
For dumplings: *2 lbs. grated potato, 3 lbs. flour, 3 lbs. suet*

Pour into the deep tins which fit the ovens. Cover with another tin and bake
slowly. Correct the consistency before serving. If cooked in a boiler, it will be
more convenient to add blended flour with the dumplings – otherwise the
thickened stew may burn.

Vegetable and milk soup; cold roast lamb, potato and green salad or mashed potato, piccalilli

FOR THE FAMILY (4)
VEGETABLE AND MILK SOUP

A bone or bacon bones   1 lb. potatoes   ½ lb. onions or meat flavouring essence
1 artichoke   ½ lb. carrots   outside stalks of celery   ½ oz. oatmeal   ½ oz. dripping
1½ pts. water   ¾ pt. milk   fresh herbs, tied in a small bunch   1 tablespoonful of
chopped parsley, shredded lettuce or finely shredded sprout or cabbage   seasoning

1. Cut up the vegetables. Cut carrot and celery finely.
2. Fry the onion in the margarine until savoury. Add all the vegetables, herbs and
oatmeal.
3. Pour in enough of the 1½ pints of water to cover the vegetables.
4. Cook until vegetables are soft.
5. Beat the thick vegetable mixture until smooth.
6. Add remainder of the water and boil up. Add the milk and heat and, lastly,
the freshly chopped parsley. Season carefully.
Note. – If the joint does not carve well, heat small pieces of meat in the well-
seasoned mashed potatoes.

FOR THE CANTEEN (100)

25 lbs. potatoes   4 lbs. or more onions or leeks, or some meat flavouring essence
2 lbs. artichokes   12 lbs. carrots   celery   6 ozs. dripping   12 ozs. oatmeal
5 gallons water   2 gallons milk   fresh herbs   chopped parsley or shredded greenstuff
Careful seasoning

Potatoes for salad, *30 lbs. with green salad or beetroot;* or for mashing, *52 lbs.*

Shepherd's pie, sprouts, coarsely grated raw carrot; steamed plum duff

FOR THE FAMILY (4)
SHEPHERDS PIE

½ lb. minced meat, raw   ½ oz. dripping   1 onion, if possible
1 oz. flour or fine oatmeal   ½ pt. potato water (rather less)   2 lbs. mashed potatoes
little pieces of fat   seasoning

1. Fry the onion until savoury, add meat and stir together.
2. Sprinkle in the flour or oatmeal and stir in the water and boil.
3. Cook very gently in the covered pan in the oven or on stove.
4. Boil and mash the potatoes. Season carefully. Spread a layer on the bottom of a greased enamel dish or Yorkshire pudding tin.
5. Spread the savoury mince on this potato and cover with another layer of potato.
6. Spread with melted fat or put on small pieces of fat and brown in the oven.
Serve with gravy.

FOR THE CANTEEN (100)

12½ lbs. raw minced meat   2 lbs. onions, if possible   6 ozs. dripping   1 gal. water or
vegetable water   1½ lbs. fine oatmeal or flour   parsley   24 lbs. sprouts
6 lbs. carrots   52 lbs. potatoes
Careful seasoning

Hot pot, stewed carrots, pickled red cabbage; cold custard (powder) sprinkled with mixture of cocoa and sugar

FOR THE FAMILY (4)
HOT POT

½ lb. breast mutton   4 ozs. lentils, soaked   2 lbs. potatoes   ½ lb. onions or meat flavouring essence   pepper and salt   dripping (very little) ½ oz. fine oatmeal or flour   ½ pint water

1. Cut the breast of mutton into small pieces, thin slices or dice, and stew it with the water, onion and seasoning for ½ hour.
2. Scrub the potatoes well and cut into slices, mix with sufficient pepper and salt, and the fine oatmeal.
3. Arrange the potatoes in layers with the meat and lentils in a pie-dish. Pour in the gravy.
4. Brush the top potatoes over with dripping, or fat skimmed from the top of the stew.
5. Cover closely with greased paper and cook for 1 hour. Remove the paper and continue baking for a ½ hour longer, until nicely browned.
Serve with gravy.

FOR THE CANTEEN (100)

16 lbs. breast of mutton   45 lbs. potatoes   7 lbs. lentils   1½ gallons water ¾ lb. oatmeal   pepper and salt   a little dripping   25 lbs. carrots   1 gallon gravy

Liver or minced meat roly poly, baked or steamed potatoes, swedes; baked milk pudding, with sultanas or jam

FOR THE FAMILY (4)
LIVER OR MINCED MEAT ROLY POLY

½ lb. raw meat mince or liver
Gravy: ¾ pt. vegetable water, 1 oz. dripping, 1 oz. flour, pepper and salt
Pastry: *6 ozs. self-raising flour, 2 ozs. fine oatmeal, 3 ozs. finely chopped suet, salt*

1. Make the gravy. Moisten the mince with a little of it. Season well.
2. Make the pastry. Roll out and spread with the meat mixture.
3. Roll up and bake for 1 hour or steam, without wrapping, for 2 hours.
Serve with gravy.

FOR THE CANTEEN (100)

12½ lbs. minced meat   1½ gallons gravy   9 lbs. self-raising flour   3 lbs. fine oatmeal
4 lbs. finely chopped suet   25 lbs. potatoes   40 lbs. swedes   6 lbs. bread

Roast beef, Yorkshire pudding, potatoes, Scotch kale; baked or stewed apples and oats

FOR THE FAMILY (4)

2 lbs. thick steak, lean brisket or suitable roasting meat

FOR THE CANTEEN (100)

36 lbs. roasting beef   1½ gallons gravy   52 lbs. potatoes   40 lbs. kale

Cold roast beef, winter or summer salad, green tomato chutney, mashed potato; jam or fruit pulp roly poly

FOR THE FAMILY (4)
SALAD

2 cooked potatoes   2 cooked carrots   1 cooked beetroot   1 bunch watercress
vinegar, sugar and nut oil for dressing

FOR THE CANTEEN (100)

40 lbs. potatoes   25 lbs. carrots   6 lbs. watercress   10 lbs. beetroot   6 lbs. bread
pepper   salt   vinegar   oil

⓫

Barley broth, <u>Cornish pasty, gravy,</u> carrots and potatoes

FOR THE FAMILY (4)
BARLEY BROTH

1 qt. water   1 lb. bones chopped, bacon bones, bacon rinds   chopped parsley
root vegetables, cut finely   2 ozs. rice or barley   herbs   pepper and salt

CORNISH PASTY

½ lb. breast mutton or beef pieces   1 onion   1 lb. potatoes   7 ozs. flour
3 ozs. fine oatmeal   4 ozs. fat   pepper and salt

Cut the mutton into *small* pieces and stew with the onion, a little water and the seasonings. Cut potato into rounds or dice. Make the pastry. Roll out and line a tin or enamel plate. Fill with raw potato and the mutton and onion. The mutton, which is fat, must be in small pieces in order that it will mix well with the potato or it may be rejected. Cover with the top crust and bake for about 1 hour. Serve with gravy.

FOR THE CANTEEN (100)
CORNISH PASTY

Filling (season well): *12½ lbs. breast mutton, 4 lbs. onions or*
leeks or soup essence, 14 lbs. potatoes, pepper and salt
Pastry: *10½ lbs. self-raising flour, 4½ lbs. fine oatmeal, 5 lbs. cooking fat or*
dripping or mixed fat   salt
Line large tins which fit the ovens
Soup: *6 gallons, 35 lbs. potatoes, 25 lbs. carrots, bread*

⓬

Soup, <u>fish salad;</u> bottled damson tart or chocolate custard

FOR THE FAMILY (4)

FISH SALAD

Canned herring, soused herring or mackerel, or any cooked fish
1 tin herrings or equivalent in fresh fish   2 lbs. potatoes   ¼ lb. watercress or beetroot
2 ozs. carrot, grated   chopped parsley   vinegar, pepper and salt
nut oil if white fish is used

50 large herrings soused, 10 tins of herrings or pilchards or
20 lbs. white fish without bone   40 lbs. potatoes   6 lbs. watercress or
2 lbs. finely shredded greenstuff   3 lbs. finely grated carrot   chopped parsley, pepper and
salt   1 pint vinegar and a little sugar   6 lbs. bread

Sea pie, greens, potatoes; rhubarb or any fruit in jelly

FOR THE FAMILY (4)
SEA PIE

Stew: *½ lb. pieces beef, 2 ozs. liver, 1 lb. carrots, celery and swede (cut in small pieces)*

Sauce: *1 oz. dripping, 1 onion, 1 oz. flour, 1 pint water, gravy colouring*

Pastry: *4 ozs. self-raising flour, 2 ozs. oatmeal, 2 ozs. suet*

1. Melt the fat and fry the onion, add flour and water.
2. Season and add meat and vegetables.
3. Stew gently for 1½ hours.
4. Make the suet pastry. Form it into a round shape to fit the pan. Note that there is plenty of gravy; if too thick, add water. Put the pastry over the stew and cook for ½ hour longer.
5. Cut the crust into sections, remove, dish the stew and serve the sections of crust on the top.
Cook this dish in a rather large pan. The pastry should not be put on too thick.

FOR THE CANTEEN (100)

Stew: *12 lbs. beef pieces, 2 lbs. liver, 24 lbs. carrots, 1 head celery, 2 swedes, if possible*

Sauce: *1 lb. dripping, 2 lbs. onions, 1½ lbs. flour, 3 gallons water*

Dumplings: *4 lbs. self-raising flour, 2 lbs. fine oatmeal, 2 lbs. finely chopped suet*

The large quantity of pastry should be made into a roly and baked or steamed separately

40 lbs. potatoes, 40 lbs. greens, 6 lbs. bread

Salad of potato, carrot, watercress, cheese, dressed with nut oil and vinegar; <u>toad-in-the-hole</u>, gravy, potatoes

FOR THE FAMILY (4)
TOAD-IN-THE-HOLE

*½ lb. minced fresh meat   2 ozs. bread, soaked and squeezed dry, or made into crumbs
chopped parsley   pepper and salt*
Batter: *1 egg, 4 ozs. flour, 1 teasp. salt, ½ pt. milk, 1 oz. dripping*

1. Mix the mince with pepper, salt and bread, shape into 4 or 8 balls or sausages.
2. Melt the fat in a Yorkshire pudding tin, put in the meat balls and baste. Cook for 10 minutes in the oven.
3. Pour in the batter and bake for a further 30 minutes until crisp and brown.

FOR THE CANTEEN (100)

*12½ lbs. raw minced meat   3 lbs. bread   3 tablesps. chopped parsley   1½ gals. milk
6 lbs. flour   18 eggs or dried egg   1 lb. dripping   seasoning   1 gallon gravy
52 lbs. potatoes   10 lbs. carrots   6 lbs. bread*

Seven suggestions for dinners which need no meat

· 1 ·
Pea vegetable and milk soup. Hard brown bread. Steamed fruit pudding.

· 2 ·
Eggs in savoury white sauce or savoury carrots. Greens. Potatoes. Apple charlotte or baked bread pudding.

· 3 ·
Potato, celery and milk soup. Curried beans and green vegetable.

Stoved potatoes, oat cakes. Stewed apple pulp, dried or fresh, and cornflour. Glass of milk.

Fresh or tinned fish, potato, beetroot and cress salad. Milk pudding and jam or sultanas.

Parsnip, carrot and potato pie, gravy, greens. Bottled plum pulp and custard. Glass of milk.

Artichoke and potato milk soup. Beetroot, cress, bean and carrot salad with sweetened dressing.

National Wheatmeal bread to be served with each meal.

Three methods of serving meals to large numbers of people may be considered:

Method 1. A given number of portions may be prepared and served as complete dishes on each table. The leaders carve the food for the seated diners. This is perhaps the most civilised method. It entails more labour in cooking and washing up and more oven space, but less labour in apportioning food.

Method 2. Portions may be collected from the source of supply by individuals. This entails a "queue" which has its disadvantages where children are concerned, but this is perhaps the best way for adults. The equipment (in ideal circumstances) should include a hot cupboard where portions of food can be kept warm.

Method 3. When the diners are seated the prefects or leaders collect the plates of food from the source of supply and serve them to their colleagues. This method works well when equipment is limited and is often adopted even when the equipment includes a hot cupboard.

CLOTHING COUPON QUIZ

Answers to Questions on the Rationing of Clothing, Footwear, Cloth and Knitting Yarn

Issued by the Board of Trade

How the Rationing Scheme works

1. There is enough for all if we share and share alike. Rationing is the way to get fair shares. *Fair shares*—when workers are producing guns, aeroplanes and bombs instead of frocks, suits and shoes. *Fair shares*—when ships must run the gauntlet with munitions and food rather than with wool and cotton. *Fair shares*—when movements of population outrun local supplies. It is *your* scheme—to defend you as a consumer and as a citizen. All honest people realise that trying to beat the ration is the same as trying to cheat the nation.

2. You must present coupons to buy clothing, cloth, footwear and knitting yarn. The coupons to be used first are the "Margarine" Coupons in your Food Ration Book issued in January, 1941. There are 26 coupons on the margarine page, and the numbers printed on them are to be ignored; each coupon counts 1 only.

3. You do not have to use up all the margarine coupons in your old Food Book by any particular date. It is much better to keep your coupons as long as possible—you should plan your needs, looking ahead a little.

4. When you have used the coupons in your old Food Book you will have to take this Book to the Post Office and exchange it for one of the new Clothing Cards with 40 coupons, making a total of 66 coupons for the full year (ending 31st May, 1942). Coupons for clothing can be used in any quantity at any time, except that when you get your new Clothing Card you will find on it 20 coupons marked X. These can only be used after 1st January, 1942. Keep your old Food Book in safety until you have used all the margarine coupons; you can then exchange it for a Clothing Card.

5. Use your coupons for whatever clothing you need—*when* you need it. You can shop anywhere without registration—the retailer will simply cut out the proper number of margarine coupons from your Food Book and give it back to you. *Do not cut the coupons out yourself.* (It is illegal to sell or buy coupons, for this would defeat the purpose of *"fair shares."*)

6. If you order goods by post, however, you must cut out the correct number of coupons yourself, sign your name clearly on the back, and send them with the order. If the retailer cannot supply you, you can either let him keep the coupons and order something else, or you can have them sent back. If you get them back they can only be used for another order by post. They will not be accepted over the counter.

7. Special cases are being looked after. Expectant mothers get a special ration to cover the baby clothes, and there is a list of infants' clothes (suitable for the "under fours") which require very little coupons. Because children grow fast their clothes are rated at less coupons than grown peoples', provided they wear clothes of types and sizes which are exempt from Purchase Tax. Children who are too big to wear these clothes will be given extra coupons. The details of this scheme will be announced later. People who have been bombed out are able to get special replacement coupons for essential clothing.

What Clothing Coupons look like

8. Illustrations of the coupons for clothing are shown here for your guidance. The examples depict single coupons, but your coupons must not be cut from the Food Book or Clothing Card by anyone except the retailer. The actual coupons you use have tinted patterned backgrounds, whilst the coupon vouchers (*d, e* and *f*), issued for special cases, are printed on tinted paper.

(*a*) shows the "margarine" coupons from your old Food Book. (*The "Butter and Margarine" coupons from the Ration Book you have for food for the period commencing July, 1941, are NOT valid for clothing*);

(*b*) and (*c*) depict the coupons on the Clothing Cards which are now ready for issue (see para. 56);

(*d*), (*e*) and (*f*) are emergency vouchers issued in 10's, 5's and 2's to people who need them for special reasons, such as the replacement of essential clothing after being bombed out.

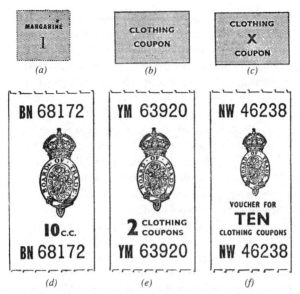

(a)   (b)   (c)

BN 68172	YM 63920	NW 46238
10 c.c.	2 CLOTHING COUPONS	VOUCHER FOR TEN CLOTHING COUPONS
BN 68172	YM 63920	NW 46238

(d)   (e)   (f)

[Numbers 9–14, which relate to the number of coupons required per item of clothing, cloth, knitting yarn, coupon-free articles and second-hand articles have been omitted here.]

Your questions answered

15. Where and when can I use my Ration Book or Clothing Card? The coupons may be used at any shop or number of shops. They may be used at any rate and at any time except for 20 out of the 40 on the Clothing Card, which will be found to be marked X and which can only be used after 1st January, 1942. The object of this is to even out the demand.

16. Are clothes of sizes suitable for babies under four rationed now? Yes, the coupon ratings are given in paragraph 10 [not included here].

17. How can men in the Services obtain clothing? The following articles of uniform may be supplied without coupons to Officers and Cadets of the Navy, Army and Air Force (including the W.R.N.S., A.T.S. and W.A.A.F.) and of the Allied Forces. These goods may also be supplied without coupons by one trade to another:—

Tunics, naval jackets and trousers, Service dress; tunics, naval jackets and trousers of khaki or white drill; skirts (when sold with tunic); greatcoats; breeches of khaki drill (when sold with tunic); shorts of khaki drill (when sold with tunic).

Officers and Cadets who are serving members of H.M. Forces, when purchasing other rationed goods, and officers of the Naval, Military and Air Force Nursing Services, when purchasing rationed goods, including articles of uniform, may for the time being obtain supplies of rationed goods by signing a statement on the back of the trader's bill that the articles mentioned represent their essential personal requirements. The rank and regiment or unit should be indicated. Officers of the R.A.F. should sign with their name, rank and personal number only. Newly commissioned officers should show the shopkeeper their calling-up papers as proof of identity.

Only Officers and Cadets who are serving members of H.M. Forces and who do not possess civilian clothing coupons may sign bills in this way. A.T.C. Officers may sign for personal *uniform* requirements only. No other Officers or Cadets may sign.

Chief and Petty Officers of the Navy, Warrant Officers of the Army and Air Force, non-commissioned officers, ratings, and other ranks of all the Services mentioned may obtain similar facilities provided that a document is attached to the bill, signed by their commanding officer (or by the officer duly authorised to act on his behalf) and testifying that the goods represent essential personal requirements of types not supplied to them by the authorities.

The statements of certificate must in all cases be signed by the officers mentioned above. Delegation of authority to sign is not permitted.

18. If I want a dress made, do I have to give up the same number of coupons whatever the amount of cloth needed may be? If you first buy the cloth and then give it back to be made up, you surrender coupons according to the yardage. If you arrange to buy the dress when it has been made, then you give 11 coupons if it is woollen and 7 if it is of other material.

19. For how long will current year coupons be valid? Both the "margarine" and Clothing Card coupons are valid at least up to 31st May, 1942.

20. What about woollen mixtures: how are they rated? Garments containing more than 15 per cent. by weight of wool are graded as "wool." This means that nearly all mixtures containing wool count as "woollen."

21. Are coupons required for knitting yarn? Yes, provided it contains more than 16 per cent. by weight from wool. "Wool" means fibre from the coat or fleece of alpaca, camel, goat, lamb, llama, rabbit, sheep, vicuna or yak, whether or not subjected to any process of manufacture or recovery.

22. What arrangements have been made regarding clothing for inmates of Institutions? A special issue of clothing coupons is to be made to institutions whose inmates have no food ration books. Institutions registered with the Ministry of Food for block food rationing, should therefore write immediately for Application Forms for coupons to the Assistant Secretary, Board of Trade (I. & M. 2), Pine Court, Bournemouth.

23. Must Coupons be demanded against women's personal cutting-out service officers? Yes.

24. What about garments not shown on the lists published in this booklet? The number of coupons required for them will, in general, be that of the nearest like garment.

25. Are Local Authorities required to surrender coupons for their purchases? No. It is sufficient for them to certify a receipt for the goods, with which the shop-keeper will provide them.

26. Are coupons required for charitable gifts of clothing? It would be unfair if people were able to receive gifts bringing them above their ration. The charitable organisation must, therefore, collect coupons and surrender them to the Board or Trade if so directed. This also applies to bazaars and sales of work (see paragraph 47).

27. By buying a suit length and lining to hand back to the tailor for making-up may I not save a coupon or so? This may be the case in some instances, but, by and large, the coupons required for lengths and lining will not be less than the number required for a suit. See also paragraph 8.

28. What happens if clothing is lost by accident? If your stock of *essential* clothing is reduced below a certain minimum as a result of loss by fire or theft or in the laundry, or in any other accidental manner, then you should apply by post on a form (CRSC. 1A) to a Collector of Customs and Excise whose address, together with the form of application, may be obtained from the nearest Information Centre of the Local Authority. Applicants are required to give on the form particulars of the essential articles of clothing and footwear they still possess, which will be taken into account in considering claims to extra coupons. Replacement coupons will not, however, be issued if the applicant still possesses sufficient articles of clothing to meet *essential* requirements.

The above procedure also applies in other exceptional cases, for example those discharged from a hospital or institution who find that their supply of clothing is below a certain minimum level.

29. Can people who have been bombed out get coupons? Yes, if their supply of essential clothing and footwear is brought below a certain level. They can obtain financial help, as well as coupons, by applying in person to the Assistance Board, or by post to a Collector of Customs and Excise, but in cases where coupons only are needed, the application should be made to a Collector of Customs and Excise (see paragraph 28). Applications to the Customs Authorities require to be accompanied by a completed form CRSC.1, obtainable from the Information Centre of any Local Authority.

30. When should coupons be detached if orders to the retailer are given by telephone? Before the goods are handed over the person delivering them must detach the correct number of coupons from the Food Book or Clothing Card.

31. Will shops sell without coupons to gain business? If they do, they and the customer seeking to evade the law in this manner will be acting contrary to the national interest and are also liable to heavy penalties (see paragraph 89). At the same time the stock of the shop will be run down, since new stocks need coupons.

32. What if my margarine coupons have been defaced by the grocer's rubber stamp? It doesn't matter. The retailer will accept them.

33. Are coupons required for presents of rationed goods sent to friends? Coupons must be surrendered when the rationed articles are first bought but coupons are not required when such articles are subsequently given away. You should on no account send loose coupons to your friends. This is an offence (see paragraph 74).

34. How do Local Authority Hospitals get their supplies? Local Authorities can purchase free of coupon (see paragraph 25).

35. Are there coupons for babies born after 1st June 1941, and before Clothing Cards were issued? The new (4th Edition) Food Book must be taken to the Food Office where the baby's Clothing Card will be available. If the Clothing Card is issued before 1st December, 1941, it will contain 40 coupons; if issued during December, 1941, January or February, 1942—30 coupons; during March, April or May, 1942—20 coupons.

36. What about clothing and footwear for prisoners of war? Arrangements have been made between the Board of Trade and the War Organisation of the British Red Cross Society and the Order of St. John to enable next-of-kin to send clothing and footwear in their quarterly parcels to prisoners of war. A fund of 40 coupons will be issued in due course to next-of-kin for the purchase of such goods, and on receipt of the parcel at the packing centre at 14 Finsbury Circus, London, E.C.2, coupons will be returned to them to maintain their fund at the 40 level. The next-of-kin must include in their parcels the shop bills and a statement of the number of coupons used for each new article, which will be compared with the schedules issued by the Board of Trade. The number of coupons to be returned to senders of parcels will be decided by the War Organisation. The next-of-kin who have already sent parcels will have their coupons refunded and will also receive the 40 coupons from the War Organisation with their next quarterly label. *No special application should be made* in such cases. Those next-of-kin who are buying for the first time should either use their own coupons, or, if this is not possible, should apply to the above address for the necessary advance. Regimental Association secretaries and organisers of prisoners of war comforts funds approved by the War Organisation are requested to write to the above address for information concerning arrangements made for them.

37. Can "Butter and Margarine" coupons from the new (4th Edition) Food Book be used for clothing? No. Only those types of coupons illustrated in paragraph 8 are valid.

38. Are coupons required for a domestic servant's uniform? Yes. For cases where the employer provides it, see paragraph 42.

39. How can one send clothing to children evacuated overseas? Children in Canada, the United States of America, Newfoundland and certain other countries will still be able to receive parcels of clothing from their parents or guardians in this country. The Children's Overseas Reception Board, 45 Berkeley Street, London, W.1, will on request issue to the parents a special ration of 66 clothing coupons to allow them to carry on with their purchases.

40. How are plimsolls defined for rationing purposes? The definition of this is "a heelless shoe of any colour with canvas upper vulcanised to a rubber sole" and includes shoes of this description which are sold as tennis shoes.

41. Are goods required for Government contracts exempt? Yes.

42. How are uniforms for bank messengers, waitresses and others engaged in civil occupations to be purchased? Traders must collect the usual number of coupons per garment for uniforms supplied to an employer for his staff. A signed statement that the coupons were obtained by him for this purpose must be furnished by the employer. The rate of collection of the necessary coupons by the employer from the employees should be arranged between employer and staff.

43. Are coupons required for rationed goods supplied on hire or hire-purchase? Rationed goods may be hired out for a period not exceeding 14 days without surrender of coupons. If, in any case, the goods are not returned the trader must furnish the Board of Trade by the 15th day of the following month with the particulars of the goods and the name and address of the person who has failed to return them. The customer will have contravened the Order if he fails to return the goods within 14 days; and the supplier, when supplying the goods, must notify the customer of this provision.

Special arrangements are being made for theatrical costumiers.

In the case of hire-purchase, coupons must be surrendered *before* the goods are delivered.

44. What about laundry replacement service? Coupons are needed for articles replaced.

For arrangements regarding *lost* articles, see paragraph 28.

45. If I get my old costume turned, do I need coupons? Only if you have a new lining will you require coupons, according to the yardage used. If no new material is used, you will need no coupons.

46. Some schools require scholars to have big outfits. Are extra coupons available for these? No special allowance is made. The schools and parents will have to get together and decide what is reasonable in the changed circumstances. By Autumn, when the school term starts, the child will have had his full 66 coupons, of which only 20 are to be reserved for use after 1st January, 1942. (See also paragraph 92.)

47. Do purchasers of goods at charity bazaars, sales of work and jumble sales have to give up coupons? Since 5th August, 1941, it has not been permissible to sell any rationed article of clothing or footwear at bazaars or sales of work without the surrender of coupons. This also applies to secondhand articles. (See paragraph 65.) All coupons thus collected should be sent, together with a statement of the exact numbers and kinds of garments sold against them, to the Area Collection Centres of the Board of Trade.

Special arrangements are being made to permit the organisers of *bona fide* bazaars, etc., to secure rationed goods for sale at subsequent bazaars.

48. Do auctioned goods require coupons? Yes, coupons must be collected by the auctioneer. (See also paragraph 49.)

49. If a retailer wishes to dispose of his business, what is the coupon position? The Board of Trade are prepared to licence the transfer of stocks of rationed goods from one retailer to another without coupons.

In cases where a retailer is giving up business and transferring it or the stocks to another retailer, the Board will also consider issuing a licence to enable him to transfer any coupons he may have on hand at the time of the sale.

50. How can district nurses obtain uniforms? Any nurse without uniform joining a District Nursing Association for duties which require indoor and/or outdoor uniform may, as an interim measure, purchase rationed goods (including piece goods) free of coupon against surrender to the trader of a certificate enumerating the requisite articles, and stating that the nurse requires them for her duties. This certificate must be signed by the Superintendent of the Association; it will then serve the trader in lieu of the equivalent number of coupons.

51. What is the position when goods are returned by the customer to the retailer as being unsuitable? The return of coupons is only permitted where the retailer agrees within 14 days of delivery to return the price of the articles originally chosen. As the returned coupons will then have been detached from the Food Book or Clothing Card, they may be used only in the same shop or for mail order purchases elsewhere.

52. Are there coupons for expectant mothers and newly-born babies? Yes, an extra allowance of 50 clothing coupons will be given to expectant mothers. These extra coupons are obtainable from the Public Health Department of the Local Authority for Maternity and Child Welfare. Certain areas of Northern Ireland have no child welfare centre, but application for the allowance may be made to the local authority.

The applicant has to get a certificate from the doctor or midwife booked to attend the confinement, or, if she attends an ante-natal clinic, from the Medical Officer of the clinic. This she should send by post or bring to the Public Health Department; if she has doubt about the address, the doctor or midwife will tell her.

The certificate may be given as soon as pregnancy can safely be diagnosed and must state the name and address of the expectant mother, her National Registration identity card number, and the approximate date when her baby will be born. If twins are born, she can obtain an extra 50 coupons by applying again to the Public Health Department with their birth certificates; if they are diagnosed with certainty beforehand, she need not wait till they are born, as in this case a double issue will be made against the medical certificate of pregnancy.

Special clothing cards of 50 coupons will be issued later (about the end of August) as soon as printing and distribution can be completed, but, to avoid holding up the scheme till then, 10 Emergency Clothing Vouchers (blue), each equivalent to 5 coupons, will be issued to those who apply earlier. These are not quite so convenient to use as single coupons, and mothers who cannot make up the extra number of coupons with these vouchers when buying a batch of materials may prefer to use some of their own coupons and keep the blue vouchers for another time when they are buying rationed goods. If they do not want to start making their baby's clothes at once or can conveniently use coupons of their own for the time being, they will find it better to wait till the special cards are available.

The special ration will not be issued to mothers of babies born before the 5th August, 1941, as they will have bought maternity clothing and some at least of the materials for their baby's clothes before rationing started.

Besides the extra ration issued to the expectant mother, a ration will be issued for the baby after its birth (see paragraph 35).

53. Should I keep my old (Third Edition) Food Book? Most emphatically yes. The Clothing Card will be issued against this Food Book which you **must** keep when it has been replaced for food purposes by the new Food Book. Keep it after you have used up the 26 margarine coupons, until you change it for a Clothing Card.

54. Can I use my coupons for my children? Yes, the members of a family may pool their coupons.

55. What do I do about coupons sent to a supplier through the post, in a mail order transaction, when he cannot supply the goods ordered? Let him know whether you will leave the coupons on deposit to meet some future purchase from him, or whether you want them back for some other mail order business. Once the coupons are cut out they can only be used for mail order.

56. How do I get a Clothing Card after using all the margarine coupons in the Food Book? The margarine page ought, on the average, to last 4½ months (26 coupons out of a year's ration of 66), but the new Clothing Card is now obtainable from the Post Office when it is required. Please don't apply for it until you need to. All the coupons from the Food Book should be used before you change it for a Clothing Card. If you have a few odd ones left and require to buy something that needs more than this number of coupons, order the article required and leave the odd coupons with your shopkeeper before you apply for the new Clothing Card.

57. What if I lose my Clothing Card? If satisfactory evidence of the loss is given, you will be able to obtain another (containing a reduced number of coupons) at one of the main Post Offices. False declaration will render the applicant liable to heavy penalties (see paragraph 89). You must, however, take every precaution not to lose your card, since you will not find it easy to get it replaced.

58. Do I have to give up coupons for mending wool? Mending wool cards or skeins of not more than ¼ ounce are coupon-free.

59. Have any arrangements been made to provide clothing for theatrical productions? A committee has been set up to consider applications for coupons and to advise the Board of Trade. Such applications should be made to The Secretary, Theatrical Industry Rationing of Clothes Committee, Faraday House, 8/10 Charing Cross Road, London, W.C.2. This also applies to amateur productions.

60. Are coupons required for new or other gift clothing distributed by the W.V.S. to persons suffering from war distress? The W.V.S. can get supplies without coupons; but when they distribute clothing, it is only fair that they should collect coupons.

61. Where may I obtain further information on clothes rationing? From Citizen's Advice Bureaux, Women's Institutes and the W.V.S. Retailers can get help on trade questions from their local Chamber of Trade or Chamber of Commerce or from their Trade Association. These bodies are thus helping to keep the rationing scheme running as smoothly as possible.

62. Are coupons used in the Isle of Man valid here? In order to enable persons resident in the Isle of Man, which is not covered by the consumer rationing scheme in force in the United Kingdom, to purchase rationed goods on the mainland, and traders in the Isle of Man to obtain fresh stocks of rationed goods from mainland suppliers, clothing coupons issued by the Isle of Man Government under the Clothing Rationing Order, 1941, may be used in the United Kingdom, and accepted as equivalent to the coupons authorised for use in the United Kingdom under the Consumer Rationing Order made by the Board of Trade. Arrangements have been made by the Isle of Man Government for the coupons authorised for use in the United Kingdom under the Consumer Rationing Order to be used and accepted in the Isle of Man.

63. Can B.V.A.C. ambulance drivers obtain rationed clothing? Pending the conclusion of long-term arrangements, drivers of the British Volunteer Ambulance Corps may obtain supplies of rationed goods by signing a statement on a copy of the trader's bill that the articles mentioned represent their essential personal uniform requirements. This signed bill will serve the trader in lieu of the equivalent number of coupons.

64. Do coupons have to be given up when I have a garment renovated and the work entails the use of materials which require coupons? Yes. The number of coupons to be surrendered depends upon the amount of material used. But the trader is permitted to do the renovation without demanding coupons if ¼ coupon or less would have been required for the material. If the fraction works out at more than ¼ but less than 1, one coupon *must* be given up. For fractions in amounts above 1, see paragraph 99.

65. Do secondhand articles require coupons? If articles are genuine secondhand goods they do not need coupons if sold at or below prices fixed in accordance with the scale shown in par. 14. A pair of men's woollen socks, for example, which would require 3 coupons if new, can only be sold as secondhand without coupons and the selling price is not more than 8*d.* per coupon, *i.e.*, 2*s.* for a pair of women's shoes which require 5 coupons if new can only be sold as secondhand without coupons if the price is not more than 1*s.* 6*d.* per coupon, *i.e.*, 7*s.* 6*d.*

66. What are the arrangements for voluntary hospitals? Supplies of rationed goods to voluntary hospitals and other hospitals not covered by other arrangements may for the time being be made by traders without coupons against a letter of certificate to the effect that the goods, which must be specified as to quantity and type, have been supplied to the institution for its use.

67. Can men's cards be used to buy women's or children's goods and vice versa? Yes, certainly, if the interchange is between members of the same family.

68. Can some of the coupons needed for an overcoat, for example, be cut from one person's card and some from another's? Yes, if the people belong to the same family.

69. When do the coupons have to be handed over in the case of Clothing Clubs, and to whom? The coupons have to be handed over to the supplier, before the goods are supplied. If the organiser of a Clothing Club wishes to obtain the goods by post, he must send the coupons before he can obtain delivery.

70. What is the procedure when the page of "Margarine" coupons has been cut out by the grocer and is still detached? Where such a page has been recovered from the grocer with whom it has been deposited, the retailer may accept coupons from this detached page *only if the rest of the Food Book is produced at the same time.*

71. Can one buy a single shoe, sock, glove, or other article from a pair for half the number of coupons? Yes, if the shopkeeper does not object.

72. Do coupons have to be given up for hats? No. Headgear is coupon-free; but scarves made up into headgear require coupons.

73. How can people who have been shipwrecked obtain clothing? Passengers will be supplied with an initial outfit of clothing or coupons by the Public Assistance Authority or the Shipwrecked Mariners' Society acting on their behalf. The cases of officers and men in the Merchant Navy and that of fishermen are dealt with in paragraph 80.

74. Am I allowed to give loose coupons to the shopkeeper in exchange for rationed goods? To offer or accept loose coupons is an offence (see paragraph 89). The only exceptions to this rule are certain special cases such as when an employer is buying uniforms for his staff (see paragraph 42), or in the case of orders by post (when the coupons should be signed on the back).

It is not permissible to give coupons by way of change. If a customer has been given strip-tickets in units of 5 or 10 coupons, by, for example, the Assistance Board, and wishes to buy a garment requiring say 7 coupons, he should make up the two coupons out of his ordinary ration card.

75. How can knitting wool in Service colours be obtained for making comforts for the Forces? The knitter must apply for registration to her local branch of the British Legion, British Legion (Women's Section), the Women's Co-operative Guild, the National Federation of Women's Institutes, or the Women's Voluntary Services for Civil Defence, or to such other nation-wide organisations as may be announced later. No person may be registered with more than one such organisation for the purpose, and on registration her Clothing Card (or old Food Book) will be endorsed with the name of the organisation with whom she is registered. The applicant must provide satisfactory evidence that she has a relation or friend in the Forces, serving away from his or her home, and must give the regimental number or unit. No one may receive more than 1½ lb. of wool in the year ending 31st August, 1942, for knitting comforts; any more wool required will have to be obtained with the knitter's own coupons.

Working parties whose members are not individually registered with any of the above-mentioned organisations will only be able to obtain coupon-free supplies of the knitting wool for comforts and the Forces if affiliated to one of the Service organisations, namely: *Navy*—(1) Depot for Knitted Garments for the Royal Navy, (2) Navy League Seafarers' Comforts Supply: *Army*—Directory of Voluntary Organisations: *Air Force*—Royal Air Force Comfort Committee.

76. What has to be done with the clothing coupons of someone who has died? They should be returned to the local Registrar of Births and Deaths with the Food Book.

77. How can discharged members of H.M. Forces (including the Nursing Services) obtain civilian clothing? They should, for the time being, apply to a Local Information Centre for Form CRSC.1A, and follow the procedure outlined in paragraph 28.

78. How can members of the Allied Red Cross obtain uniform clothing? Pending the conclusion of long-term arrangements, uniformed personnel of recognised Allied Red Cross Committees may now purchase coupon-free uniform clothing on (*a*) presenting to the shop a Red Cross membership card, (*b*) signing a statement on the back of the trader's bill that the goods represent essential personal requirements of uniform and (c) giving after the signature the address of the Red Cross Committee concerned and the unit number (if any) of the member.

The Allied Red Cross Committees recognised by the British Red Cross are the Belgian, Czechoslovakia, Netherland, Norwegian and Polish Red Cross Committees in London. The bill as signed above will serve the retailer in lieu of coupons.

79. Must I give coupons when I buy cloth for household furnishing? This is rationed, but certain furnishing fabrics may be sold without coupons to members of the public. These can be bought from the retailer either by the yard, or made-up, or made-to-measure (see paragraph 13). For sheets, towels, dusters, etc., see paragraph 88.

80. How do men in the Merchant Navy and fishermen obtain their clothing? Arrangements have been made for the supply without coupons of clothing to officers and men of the Merchant Navy and fishermen who are in need of this clothing for service at sea or who have been shipwrecked. Particulars of these arrangements can be obtained at Mercantile Marine offices, but retailers should note that for the present they may sell clothes and footwear without the surrender of coupons against certificates issued by superintendents of Mercantile Marine offices. Shipwrecked mariners may apply alternatively to the Shipwrecked Mariners' Society.

81. What is the position regarding the supply of rationed uniform clothing to Members of the British Red Cross Society, St. John Ambulance Brigade and Members of the War Organisation of the British Red Cross Society and Order of St. John, including trained nurses, also the Members of the Women's Transport Service (F.A.N.Y.)? Members of these Organisations may obtain their essential personal requirements of rationed uniform clothing and footwear without coupons during the period until final arrangements have been made to provide them with supplies of clothing coupons.

Officers and Members of the British Red Cross Society, of the St. John Ambulance Brigade and Officers of the War Organisation of the B.R.C.S. and Order of St. John may obtain supplies of rationed goods by signing a statement on the back of the trader's bill that the articles mentioned represent their essential personal uniform requirements. Trained nurses of the War Organisation B.R.C.S. and Order of St. John may obtain similar facilities. The rank of the Officer or Member and the County and number of Detachment should be shown in the case of the B.R.C.S. and in the case of the St. John Ambulance Brigade the rank of the Officer or Member and the County and name of the Division must be given. Trained Nurses of the War Organisation must intimate their membership of that body.

Non-commissioned Officers and men of the War Organisation will continue to obtain supplies of uniform from the Uniform Department of the War Organisation.

The Officers of the Women's Transport Service (F.A.N.Y.) Corps Units may obtain supplies of rationed goods by signing a statement on the back of the trader's bill that the articles mentioned represent their essential personal uniform requirements. The rank and unit should be indicated. Non-commissioned Officers and other ranks may obtain similar facilities provided that a document is attached to the bill signed by the Officer-in-Charge, Women's Transport Service (F.A.N.Y.) Headquarters, testifying that the goods represent essential personal uniform requirements.

82. What about civilian personnel employed with H.M. Forces? Until military clothing coupons are issued, retailers are authorised to supply civilian personnel paid by and attached to Army establishments or units, and who are supplied with rationed foodstuffs by the Army authorities and thus have no civilian ration cards, with their essential personal requirements of clothing, provided these are detailed on a document signed by the Commanding Officer of the unit concerned and bearing its office stamp. The document will be surrendered to the retailer at the time of purchase.

83. What arrangements are there for manual workers who, because of the nature of their employment, wear out their clothing and footwear more quickly than other people, and of those who require protective clothing? Industrial concerns, including mines and quarries, can now purchase for their employees types of overalls which are not exempt from the Consumer Rationing Order and other protective clothing and footwear, necessary for safety or health, without coupons. Concerns wanting to avail themselves of this arrangement must obtain a certificate from one of H.M. Inspectors of Factories or Mines stating that the clothing, the nature and quantities of which must be specified, is required for safety and health. This certificate is from the trader's point of view equivalent to the number of coupons for the clothing.

Other cases mentioned in the question are still under consideration by the Board in consultation with the industries concerned.

84. May a person entering H.M. Forces give his coupons to members of his family or to any other person? No. He has to surrender them to the responsible Naval, Military or Air Force Authorities.

85. Are coupons required for orders given before 1st June, 1941? These require coupons, even if a deposit has been paid.

86. Is it permissible for relatives of a family to pool their coupons with those of the family so as to give a bride a trousseau? Yes but remember that the Ration Books or Clothing Cards must be taken to the shop whenever purchases are made and coupons must only be cut out by the retailer.

87. Won't I run short of clothing next winter? Not if you PLAN the use of your coupons. You will have 66 coupons for the year in all, 26 of them in your January-June, 1941, Food Book, 40 when you get your Clothing Card. Think over your general needs for the year and decide how you may best spread the ration. You should allow for winter needs and leave coupons over for casual purchases.

88. Are such things as sheets, serviettes and table-cloths rationed? Ready-made household textile articles are not rationed, but if you buy stuff in the piece to make up yourself, or have it made up to your own requirements, it is rationed and needs coupons (see also paragraph 79).

89. May I sell coupons I don't need, or may I buy other people's spare coupons? No, it is illegal and subject to heavy penalties. (On summary conviction for a contravention of the Consumer Rationing Orders, a person may be imprisoned for 3 months or fined up to £100, or both. On conviction on indictment the penalty is up to two years' imprisonment or a fine not exceeding £500, or both.)

90. What is the position regarding cut rug wool? All knitting wool is rationed; if wool, therefore, can be used for knitting, coupons are required for it; if, however, it is cut into small pieces, and it is impossible to use it for knitting purposes, it can be sold free of coupons.

91. Collar attached to shirt—how many coupons are needed for this? Collars sold separately require coupons, but a shirt with collar attached counts as a shirt and requires 7 coupons if woollen and 5 if made of other material for adults' sizes, and 6 and 4 respectively for children's sizes.

92. What provision has been made for the fact that growing children require a good many clothes? The number of coupons for articles of children's clothing and footwear is lower than that for adults. For those children who are too big to wear children's sizes, extra coupons will be issued and the details will be published later.

93. Children under four are often as big as those of six or seven. Are coupons needed for their ready-made clothes according to the children's or to the infants' scale? The test is size and not age in these cases.

94. If I buy goods with "thrift tickets" or other tokens in lieu of cash, are coupons required? Yes, because in fact coupons are required whenever rationed goods are *supplied*.

95. Are furs rationed? Fur skins are unrationed, but fur ties require 5 coupons (5 coupons *per skin* in the case of fox-fur ties) and fur coats are rated as coats, according to their size. All other garments of fur or imitation fur are rationed.

96. What if I make my own clothes? If you are of average size and choose economical patterns you should gain slightly by making your own clothes, especially skirts and blouses. You can save considerably by making clothes for children aged four to seven.

97. Is there any allowance for socks and shirts for officers and other ranks of the Home Guard and A.T.C.? There is no special allowance as they already have the full ration of coupons for their current requirements.

98. When goods are sent out on approval, must coupons be surrendered? Rationed goods may be supplied on approval without coupons for a period not exceeding 14 days provided the customer first states the quantity and description of the goods he desires to purchase, and surrenders the appropriate number of coupons. A woman ordering a woollen skirt, for instance, must send 6 coupons. The trader can then send a selection of skirts from which the customer can make her choice. If she does not return the unselected skirts within 14 days, the trader must send particulars to the Board of Trade by the fifteenth day of the following month.

If more goods are kept than were originally intended, the appropriate number of coupons must be sent.

99. What happens when the number of coupons to be given up includes a fraction? Coupons must in no circumstances be cut into pieces. The fraction should be made up to the nearest whole number if it is half or more. If it is less than a half, it should be ignored, except that where the number comes to less than 1, it counts as 1; *e.g.*, $5\frac{1}{2}$ or $5\frac{2}{3}$ counts as 6, $5\frac{1}{3}$ counts as 5, but $\frac{1}{3}$ counts as 1. For the purpose of finding exactly how many coupons should be given up, all purchases made at the same time should be added together, *e.g.*, a yard of 54-in. wool cloth sold at the same time as a large handkerchief make $4\frac{1}{2}$ plus $\frac{1}{2}$, which equals 5 coupons.

100. Does a gift of clothing to a charitable institution require coupons? If you buy rationed goods to give to a charitable institution you must surrender coupons for their purchase, but no coupons have to be handed over by the institution authorities when they receive these gifts.

CHAPTER 2
EVACUATION

EVACUATION WHY AND HOW?
Public Information Leaflet No.3

Read this and keep it carefully. You may need it.

Issued from the Lord Privy Seal's Office July, 1939

Why Evacuation?

There are still a number of people who ask "What is the need for all this business about evacuation? Surely if war comes it would be better for families to stick together and not go breaking up their homes?"

It is quite easy to understand this feeling, because it is difficult for us in this country to realise what war in these days might mean. If we were involved in war, our big cities might be subjected to determined attacks from the air—at any rate in the early stages—and although our defences are strong and are rapidly growing stronger, some bombers would undoubtedly get through.

We must see to it then that the enemy does not secure his chief objects—the creation of anything like panic, or the crippling dislocation of our civil life.

One of the first measures we can take to prevent this is the removal of the children from the more dangerous areas.

The Government Evacuation Scheme

The Government have accordingly made plans for the removal from what are called "evacuable" areas (see list at the back of this leaflet) to safer places called "reception" areas, of school children, children below school age if accompanied by their mothers or other responsible persons, and expectant mothers and blind persons.

The scheme is entirely a voluntary one, but clearly the children will be much safer and happier away from the big cities where the dangers will be greatest.

There is room in the safer areas for these children; householders have volunteered to provide it. They have offered homes where the children will be made welcome. The children will have their schoolteachers and other helpers with them and their schooling will be continued.

What You Have To Do

Schoolchildren

Schoolchildren would assemble at their schools when told to do so and would travel together with their teachers by train. The transport of some 3,000,000 in all is an enormous undertaking. *It would not be possible to let all parents know in advance the place to which each child is to be sent but they would be notified as soon as the movement is over.*

If you have children of school age, you have probably already heard from the school or the local education authority the necessary details of what you would have to do to get your child or children taken away. *Do not hesitate to register your children under this scheme, particularly if you are living in a crowded area.* Of course it means heartache to be separated from your children, but you can be quite sure that they will be well looked after. That will relieve you of one anxiety at any rate. You cannot wish, if it is possible to evacuate them, to let your children experience the dangers and fears of air attack in crowded cities.

Children under five

Children below school age must be accompanied by their mothers or some other responsible person. Mothers who wish to go away with such children should register with the Local Authority. *Do not delay in making enquiries about this.*

A number of mothers in certain areas have shown reluctance to register. Naturally, they are anxious to stay by their menfolk. Possibly they are thinking that they might as well wait and see; that it may not be so bad after all. *Think this over carefully and think of your child or children in good time.* Once air attacks have begun it might be very difficult to arrange to get away.

Expectant Mothers

Expectant mothers can register at any maternity or child welfare centre. For any further information inquire at your Town Hall.

The Blind

In the case of the Blind, registration to come under the scheme can be secured through the home visitors, or enquiry may be made at the Town Hall.

Private Arrangements

If you have made private arrangements for getting away your children to relatives or friends in the country, or intend to make them, you should remember that while the Government evacuation scheme is in progress ordinary railway and road services will necessarily be drastically reduced and subject to alteration at short notice. Do not, therefore, in an emergency leave your private plans to be carried out at the last moment. It may then be too late.

If you happen to be away on holiday in the country or at the seaside and an emergency arises, do not attempt to take your children back home if you live in an "evacuable" area.

Work Must Go On

The purpose of evacuation is to remove from the crowded and vulnerable centres, if an emergency should arise, those, more particularly the children, whose presence cannot be of any assistance.

Everyone will realise that there can be no question of wholesale clearance. We are not going to win a war by running away. Most of us will have work to do, and work that matters, because we must maintain the nation's life and the production of munitions and other material essential to our war effort. For most of us therefore, who do not go off into the Fighting Forces our duty will be to stand by our jobs or those new jobs which we may undertake in war.

Some people have asked what they ought to do if they have no such definite work or duty.

You should be very sure before deciding that there is really nothing you can do. There is opportunity for a vast variety of services in civil defence. YOU must judge whether in fact you can or cannot help by remaining. If you are sure you cannot, then there is every reason why you should go away if you can arrange to do so, but you should take care to avoid interfering with the official evacuation plans. If you are proposing to use the public transport services, make your move either BEFORE the evacuation of the children begins or AFTER it has been completed. You will not be allowed to use transport required for the official evacuation scheme and other essential purposes, and you must not try to take accommodation which is required for the children and mothers under the Government scheme.

For the rest, we must remember that it would be essential that the work of the country should go on. Men and women alike will have to stand firm, to maintain our effort for victory. Such measures of protection as are possible are being pushed forward for the large numbers who have to remain at their posts. That they will be ready to do so, no one doubts.

The "evacuable" areas under the Government scheme are:—

(*a*) London, as well as the County Boroughs of West Ham and East Ham; the Boroughs of Walthamstow, Leyton, Ilford and Barking in Essex; the Boroughs of Tottenham, Hornsey, Willesden, Acton, and Edmonton in Middlesex; (*b*) The Medway towns of Chatham, Gillingham and Rochester; (*c*) Portsmouth, Gosport and Southampton; (*d*) Birmingham and Smethwick; (*e*) Liverpool, Bootle, Birkenhead and Wallasey; (*f*) Manchester and Salford; (*g*) Sheffield, Leeds, Bradford and Hull; (*h*) Newcastle and Gateshead; (*f*) Edinburgh, Rosyth, Glasgow, Clydebank and Dundee.

In some of these places only certain areas will be evacuated. Evacuation may be effected from a few other places in addition to the above, of which notice will be given.

EVACUATION

DETAILS OF FACILITIES ARRANGED FOR

(1) OFFICIAL PARTIES
(TO BILLETS PROVIDED BY THE GOVERNMENT)

Evacuation is available for

SCHOOL CHILDREN
MOTHERS with CHILDREN of School Age or under
EXPECTANT MOTHERS

(2) ASSISTED PRIVATE EVACUATION
A free travel voucher and billeting allowance are provided for

CHILDREN OF SCHOOL AGE or under
MOTHERS with CHILDREN OF SCHOOL AGE OR UNDER
EXPECTANT MOTHERS
AGED and BLIND PEOPLE
INFIRM and INVALIDS

who have made their own arrangements with relatives
or friends for accommodation in a safer area

★ *FOR INFORMATION ASK AT THE NEAREST SCHOOL*

ISSUED BY THE MINISTRY OF HEALTH

WAR TIME PLAY SCHEMES
FOR CHILDREN

One of the problems of evacuation is how to occupy the children out of school hours and relieve the householders. If a child is idle he will either be unhappy or get into mischief. If he can be given something congenial and useful to do, it will be good for him and the greatest help to those with whom he is living. This leaflet gives some hints on how this may be brought about.

Getting Things Done

Everyone's job is sometimes nobody's job. Some villages have welfare committees, some have Boy Scouts, Girl Guides or similar Youth Organisations. But others have none; and here anyone who has the time and aptitude can get things going if a start is made in the right way. Those who should first of all be consulted are the teachers, both local and visiting, and the juvenile organisations. Teachers are not legally required to look after the children out of school hours, but they look beyond their immediate job and should always be asked to help. There will be need, too, to consult with officials. Out-of-school activities concern not only the local education authority but also (in so far as they are for evacuated children) the authority responsible for evacuation arrangements, i.e., the Borough, Urban or Rural District Council.

Play Rooms

Many halls have been taken over for war purposes but the authorities have been urged by the Ministry of Health and the Board of Education to try to arrange for at least one hall in each place to be available for social purposes. Sometimes the school can be used. If it would have to be "blacked out" before it could be used for recreation after dark, and the Education Authority was unwilling to do this because it was not necessary for its own work, the Council might be asked whether the work could be done as an evacuation charge. In many places rooms and equipment will be offered free, but if some money is essential to start the scheme the Council will be able to advise whether any help could be given from evacuation funds. Everyone realises how necessary it is to save public funds and to make shift as far as possible.

Management and Finance

A small representative committee to run the scheme is suggested unless an existing organisation is taking it on. This committee would appoint a leader, plan the hours of opening and programmes, and deal with any financial questions.

Leaders

Leaders must like the job and be able to organise, and should have had experience with groups of children. In most cases they will be found locally, but if there is no-one in a particular place with the time and ability, the Ministry of Health would consider an application from the Local Authority to pay a billeting allowance for a helper with special qualifications. The Central Council of Recreative Physical Training has a national register of leaders from which it may be able to suggest suitable leaders. Further, the Council has two technical representatives working for each Civil Defence Region, who as far as other duties allow will gladly act in an advisory capacity. All correspondence should be addressed to the Headquarters of the C.C.R.P.T., Abbey House, Victoria Street, London, S.W.1. Remember, too, that many local Education Authorities employ physical training organisers. Their advice would be invaluable, and it would be wise to get into touch with them.

Hints on Programme Planning

These can only be very general, but the list of books given on the back [not included here] will be found useful.

1. Plan the activities to include both local and visiting children.

2. Try and plan a separate scheme for your younger and older children. They might come on different days.

3. Divide the children, if possible, into two groups: a quiet play group and an active play group. Change them over every hour or half-

hour. A leader is needed for each group and a pianist is a great help for the active group.

4. If there are enough rooms use a separate one for each kind of activity, e.g., handicrafts, reading room, games rooms.

5. As a rough guide 50–60 children can be occupied in a room 60 x 30 feet.

6. In some places there may be people willing to entertain a small group of children in their own houses for one or two nights a week. This is specially valuable where a large playroom is not available.

7. Arrange for escorts where necessary.

NOTES AND SUGGESTIONS ON CLOTHING

for those caring for unaccompanied children in the reception areas

Householders—

(*a*) are not expected to provide clothes, but are responsible for the care and washing of the clothes of children in their homes. In many places mending parties and voluntary laundries have been started to help the individual housewife.

(*b*) are asked to look ahead and report to the teacher, billeting officer or welfare committee in good time when new clothes are becoming necessary and also when shoes are likely to need repairing.

(*c*) are not entitled to spend money on the children and send the bill to the parents unless the parents have said they may beforehand.

Teachers, Billeting Officers and Welfare Committees

are asked to work in close contact one with another and to arrange between themselves who shall

(*a*) . . . write to the parents concerning new clothes for the child.

(*b*) . . . write to the Education or Local Authority in the area from which the child has been evacuated, asking them to arrange for the parents to be visited, *should the parents not respond.*

(*c*) . . . report to the Education Authority in the area from which the child has been evacuated if boots and shoes are urgently needed and are not forthcoming from the parents. Full particulars of the child should be sent:—

1. Name of child.
2. Name of school from which he came.
3. Address in the reception area.
4. Size of shoes.

The following should be noted:—

1. Welfare Committees normally should not make gifts of clothes from voluntary sources until they are assured after a report on a visit to the child's own home that the parents cannot provide clothing.

2. In writing to parents about new clothes they should be reminded that their children will need warmer and harder-wearing clothes and stronger footwear than at home, because they will be walking on wet and muddy roads and running about among trees and bushes. They do not need smart clothes, but should have sensible jerseys, strong boots, or shoes or Wellingtons, and a waterproof.

3. If a good scheme for buying locally has been started, parents may be glad to send money for suitable boots or clothes to be bought where the child can be fitted.

What the Child Needs

It is important that the parents should not be asked to send more than is reasonable. Difficulty has sometimes occurred because householders, accustomed to a higher standard of living, have asked for a greater range of clothing than the child's mother has been used to buying, and the following suggestions are for general guidance. All children possess some of the articles specified, and parents cannot, of course, be asked to make up deficiencies all at once.

Footwear—a pair of strong boots or shoes or Wellingtons and a pair of plimsolls or slippers. (It is an economy if both boots or shoes *and* Wellingtons can be provided, as Wellingtons can then be kept for wet days and boot leather prevented from getting soaked.)

Coats—if possible an over-coat and mackintosh in order to save the mackintosh.

Stockings or Socks—at least three pairs.

Underclothes—a change of underclothing including vests and pants for boys and vests and knickers for girls, also a change of nightclothes.

Shorts and Jerseys or Suits for boys, Skirts and Jumpers or Frocks for girls—a change and an extra jersey or a cardigan for cold weather is desirable.

Miscellaneous—handkerchiefs, comb, toothbrush, and face-flannel.

Issued by the
Women's Group on Problems arising from Evacuation
(In association with the National Council for Social Service) through
THE WOMEN'S VOLUNTARY SERVICES
FOR CIVIL DEFENCE

MINISTRY OF HEALTH
WHITEHALL, S.W.1

You are among the many fathers and mothers who wisely took advantage of the Government's scheme to send their children to the country. I am sorry to learn that some parents are now bringing their children back.

I am writing to ask you not to do this. This is not easy, for family life has always been the strength and pride of Britain. But I feel it my duty to remind you that to bring children back to the Congested towns is to put them in danger of death or that is perhaps worst, maiming for life.

You will have noticed that the enemy is changing his tactics.

He is now concentrating heavier air raids on one or two towns at a time, leaving others alone for the moment.

Nobody knows which town he will attack next. So don't be lulled into a false sense of security if your home district has been having a quieter time lately.

Remember that in April over 600 children under sixteen were killed and over 500 seriously injured in air raids.

So keep your children where they are in the reception areas.

Don't bring them back now for a little while. This is your duty to the children themselves, to the A.R.P. Services in your home town, to those who are working so hard for them in the country, and to the nation.

I know that at times you feel lonely without your children and, believe me, I sympathise with you.

But you know as well as I do that it is far better to feel lonely now than to take a risk you may regret for the rest of your life.

Please read this message as the sincere words of a friend both to you and to the little ones.

Yours sincerely,

Ernest Brown.

June 1941

CHAPTER 3

CONSCRIPTION

THE C.O.
THE TRIBUNAL AND AFTER
A Guide For Conscientious Objectors,
Explaining Their Rights and Status under
The National Service (Armed Forces) Act.

Edited and compiled by Guy A. Aldred, on behalf of The Advisory
Bureau, of The Glasgow and West of Scotland, No-Conscription
League, Glasgow, 1940

The purpose of this pamphlet is to define the status and rights,
under the National Service Armed Forces Act, of conscientious
objectors. The Act permits such men to apply to Tribunals for
exemption on the grounds of conscience. Many conscientious objectors
refuse to apply to such Tribunals on the ground that no Tribunal can
decide a man's conscience. Sir John Simon, now Chancellor of the
Exchequer, and a member of the present War Cabinet, took this view
in a speech he made in the House of Commons, on January 12, 1916,
when opposing conscription during the last war. It is a perfectly sound
view. Those who take this view face arrest, handing over to the Military
authorities by the magistrate, and trial by Court Martial without being
heard by Tribunals. They can arrange for their friends to sign, at the
proper time, Form D and forward to the Secretary of the N.C.L.
(Glasgow and West of Scotland District). After the Military
Authorities take action, the N.C.L., if kept in touch, will do all it can
to safeguard their rights and vindicate their stand for conscience.

This pamphlet is not addressed immediately to those who take this
uncompromising stand. It's purpose is to advise those who intend to
state their case before the Tribunals set up under the National Service
(Armed Forces) Act, 1939.

Who Are Liable For Service?

All male British subjects between the ages of 18 and 41, who are within the age-groups fixed from time to time by Royal Proclamation, or subsequently enter it.

[Certain British subjects who do not belong to Great Britain, employed by the Government outside of Great Britain, clergymen and regular ministers of any denomination, mental patients, mentally defective persons and blind persons are exempt.]

The procedure for calling-up is as follows. A person within the age groups fixed by Royal Proclamation must register at the local Labour Exchange on the date fixed as the registration date.

Your Rights Under the Act

(1) REGISTRATION:— If you object to being conscripted for war you have the **LEGAL** right under Section 5 of the Act to be registered in the **SPECIAL REGISTER FOR CONSCIENTIOUS OBJECTORS.**

(On another page, Form A explains exactly what you have to do on registration day [not included here].)

Having registered as a conscientious objector, you are entered provisionally on the Register of Conscientious Objectors.

(2) THE NEXT STEP:— Within 14 days of registration you must make application on the form provided to a Local Tribunal. The application must state to which of the three items mentioned in the National Service Act he objects:–

(1) to being registered in the Military Service Register;
(2) to performing military duties;
(3) to performing combatant duties.

You are required to delete whichever item does not apply. You do not strike out the item against which your objection is directed. This is a very confusing enactment and **my advice is to strike out none of these items.** Before accepting this advice, you should consider the matter very carefully. Most objectors strike out items (2) and (3) and leave item (1).

71

They consider that objection to this item defines complete objection to military service. Here are their reasons.

The Tribunal may dismiss your application and order your name to be placed on the Military Service Register without qualification. This means that it does not consider that you are a genuine conscientious objector, in the full legal sense of the term. This decision does not imply in every instance, a censure. The Tribunal is at pains, sometimes to explain this fact. It may mean that your objection is intellectual rather than moral and is not rooted, sufficiently, in your being.

Apart from total rejection, the Tribunal is empowered by the Act to give one of three decisions:–

(1) Unconditional exemption.

(2) exemption conditional on the applicant agreeing until the end of the present emergency to undertake work as specified by the tribunal, but of a civil character and under civilian control.

(3) placing on the non-combatant section of the Military Service Register.

These three decisions are intended, apparently, to correspond with the three objections defined above. If you object to being registered in the Military Service Register, you should obtain unconditional exemption, if the Tribunal decides that you have made out your case for conscience. If your objection is to military duties, then conditional exemption must be the decision. If you object to performing combatant duties, obviously non-combatant work is the solution.

I feel, however, the items of objection are not defined well. I think the absolutist should register his objections to all 3 items by deleting none. My advice to him is to make no statement on his form, other than one to the following effect:

"I have not deleted any of the items (a), (b) or (c). My reason is that I claim total exemption. Item (a) could define the nature of my objection but as I object to each item, I prefer to delete none. I have not stated my reasons for claiming exemption on this form. I am prepared to do so before the Tribunal".

This should be the substance of the statement. Using a set form of words ought not to worry any conscientious objector. At this stage of

72

proceedings, the entire process is formal. If the Tribunal endeavours to make a point of this statement being similar to some other statement, the answer is that this form is filled in only to secure a hearing, as a prelude. **Your statement to the Tribunal is your plea for exemption when you appear to say why you are a conscientious objector.**

What the Decisions Mean

The Tribunal may order your name to be placed on the Military Register without qualification, or it may grant you one of three kinds of exemption. It is necessary for you to understand what these exemptions mean:-

(1) Unconditional Exemption.

This decision is given rarely. The persons to whom it is intended to apply have been defined best by the Bristol and the Manchester Tribunals. It is reserved for persons who convince the Tribunals of their sincerity and obduracy. Men obtaining total exemption satisfy the Tribunal they are prepared to do nothing **under the Act** for one, two, or all of the following reasons:–

(1) They feel called upon to use this opportunity of witnessing against war in general, or of this war in particular, because they are convinced of the fundamental moral error, futility, and wrong of the resort to killing and destruction.

(2) They are prepared under certain conditions, such as an epidemic or a plague, to do work acceptable to the Tribunals as a condition of exemption; but they cannot accept such work as an alternative to serving in the Forces, because they do not and cannot recognise any form of military service as a duty. This is an objection to military conscription, and may be a moral objection distinct from the moral objection to war itself.

(3) They are engaged in work that they consider vital to society and to progress, and are not prepared to accept the Tribunal decision that it is less vital to the community than some kind of work imposed as an alternative to military service.

(2) Conditional Exemption.

Exemption on condition of undertaking work of national importance, of a civil character and under civilian control.

I define the men whom it is intended to cover. They are found unwilling to act within the military machine, but prepared, to varying extents, to accept civilian work regarded as of importance in time of war. They may be divided into three classes:–

(a) Those who accept work **important only** in war-time to the community, in spite of the fact that they realise and regret that such work may give indirect assistance to the war-economy of the country. Forestry and agriculture, etc.

(b) Those who will do work of a general social value not essential to the war-machine. Teaching, social care, etc.

(c) Those who accept work **important only** in war-time but of a civilian character, or under civilian control.

These three categories of conditional exemption connect those who claim or obtain unconditional exemption with those who undertake what amounts, almost, to non-combatant service.

The third category divides into two:–

(a) Those who are willing to undertake civilian defensive work, such as A.R.P., A.F.S., Civilian First Aid, etc. [My view is that no conscientious objector should engage in such work. I view this as war preparation and activity. It is argued that, once war is started such activity is essential for the well-being of civilians. Think and decide]

(b) Those who will accept any work to which the description work of national importance applies. The Tribunals place usually within this category men who make shells, etc. [My view is that a man who makes shells or is engaged similarly, is **not** a conscientious objector.]

(3) Military Service Register: Non-Combatant Service.

Intended to cover men who are not prepared actually to kill but who do not object to being within the Forces in a non-combatant capacity. This class can be divided into:

(a) those who do not mind what they do, so long as they do not kill personally;

(b) those who are prepared to alleviate suffering in the R.A.M.C., etc., but who will not take part in killing as direct as, for example, helping to transport shells.

A limited number of non-combatant c.os may be posted to the R.A.M., Pay, Veterinary, or Dental Corps. The remainder will be posted to the Non-Combatant Labour Corps. The latter will be required to perform, in addition to normal administrative duties, special labour duties, such as:

(a) Construction of Military recreation grounds.

(b) Improvement of camping sites.

(c) Drainage of training areas.

(d) Agricultural work, e.g. the growing of crops for consumption by the troops.

(e) Filling in of trenches.

In addition, non-combatant c.os., irrespective of the corps to which they are posted, will all receive training in:

(a) Fort drill without arms.

(b) Physical Culture.

(c) Passive Air Defence.

(d) Anti-gas.

Appeals and After

If you are dissatisfied with the decision of the Local Tribunal, you can appeal within 21 days. The Appellant should fill in the special form provided. The decision of the Appellate Tribunal is final.

If finally refused exemption by the Appellate Tribunal; or, if granted work of national importance, and insisting on total exemption; the Conscientious Objector is liable to have his name removed from the Conscientious Objectors' Register. In this event, arrest may follow, and Court Martials begin. By keeping in touch with the N.C.I., the Objector will be advised and his interests protected at this stage, on to the end of his struggle against militarism in defence of conscience.

National Service (Armed Forces Act) 1939

Advice to C.O.'s Summarised.

1. Do not register until the issue of a proclamation calling up your own age group.

2. Register at your nearest Labour Exchange.

3. When registering take with you your National Registration Identity Card, and where necessary your Unemployment Card.

4. When at the Labour Exchange make it clear that you wish to be provisionally registered on the Register of C.O.'s.

5. Be sure to return your statement giving the grounds of your appeal within the prescribed time limit, usually 14 days.

6. If you decide to appeal against the decision of the Tribunal, your appeal must be submitted within 21 days.

7. If handed over to the Military, and sentenced by Court Martial to more than three months, apply to the Appeal Tribunal. The latter may order your discharge at the expiration of your sentence, and then make some order concerning your treatment as a C.O.

8. Keep in direct touch, through your relatives or friends with the N.C.L.

To Those Wishing to Appeal

1. You have an unrestricted right of appeal from the decision of a local tribunal. The Ministry of Labour has a similar right.

2. You will receive by post brief notes of the evidence in your local tribunal case. Read these carefully.

3. You should appeal on the prescribed form to the Appellate Tribunal within 21 days of the order of the local tribunal.

4. The Grounds of Appeal should include:—

(a) a clear statement of the reasons for not accepting the decision of the local tribunal;

(b) a brief re-statement of the objector's conscientious case in so far as the local tribunal has not accepted it;

(c) a clear statement of the degree of exemption the objector is prepared to accept.

If you disagree with the report of the evidence at the local tribunal carefully point out where.

The actual hearing of the case may be quite brief. Keep your written statement brief, clear and complete. Do not rely on questions by the tribunal which may or may not be put.

5. The Appellate Tribunal may dismiss the appeal or may award a greater or lesser degree of exemption.

6. Before the hearing takes place the Ministry will ask the appellant to complete a form stating whether he intends to be present in person at the hearing or whether he wishes to send in a written statement only; whether he intends to be represented at the hearing, and, if so, by whom he will be represented. This form should be completed and returned. The appellant should make a copy for his own use.

Make a point of being present at the hearing. This is both courtesy and commonsense once you have appealed to the Tribunal.

You may be represented by counsel, by a solicitor, by a representative of any trade union to which you belong, or by any person who satisfies the tribunal that he is a relative or personal friend.

7. You are entitled to call witnesses who are prepared to testify to the genuineness of your views.

A witness whose attendance is certified as necessary by the Appellate Tribunal is entitled to payment of travelling and subsistence expenses. After the decision has been given application for a certificate for the expenses of any witnesses should be made.

Appellants are entitled to travelling and subsistence expenses.

8. If witnesses cannot attend, the Tribunal will accept as evidence letters testifying to the conscientious objection of the appellant. These should be sent by post shortly before the hearing, or produced at the hearing and handed to the Tribunal members.

9. The customary form of procedure is for the appellant's "Grounds of Appeal" to be first read. The Tribunal has before it the appellant's original statement, and a copy of the evidence at the local tribunal. The appellant is then asked whether he wishes to add anything to what he has stated. If the appellant intends to call witnesses or produce letters he should indicate this.

10. The decision of the Appellate Tribunal is final.

CHAPTER 4
AIR RAIDS

YOUR HOME AS AN AIR RAID SHELTER
Issued by the Ministry of Home Security, 1940

Introduction

When a high explosive bomb falls and explodes a number of things happen. Anything very close to the explosion is likely to be destroyed, and any house which suffers a direct hit is almost sure to collapse. Fortunately, the zone of destruction within which this danger exists is very small; but other dangers of a less spectacular kind can cause far more casualties than direct hits. These are the dangers from blast and splinters of the bomb case. Blast can shatter unprotected windows at considerable distance and fragments of glass can be deadly, while bomb splinters can fly and kill at a distance of over half a mile if there is nothing to stop them. This is where your house comes in. You may have seen pictures of shattered houses and have thought that a house is no place for you; but you must not be deceived by the pictures; houses do not collapse unless the bomb falls on them or very close to them, and the chances of your house being the unlucky one are very small. In fact houses afford a great deal of protection against blast and splinters— as well as against aerial machine-gun fire and splinters of anti-aircraft shell, the dangers of which you must not underrate—and they can easily be made to afford much more. It is the object of this pamphlet to tell householders how best to go about it.

There are three ways in which you can provide your household with shelter. First, you can buy a ready-made shelter to bury or erect in the garden. Secondly, you can have a shelter of brick and concrete built into or attached to the house. Thirdly, you can improve the natural protection given by your house by forming a "refuge room." The first two of these generally give better protection against bomb splinters than the third, but cost more; they may be the only way of getting proper protection if your house is very lightly built, say of timber. A properly-prepared refuge room can, however, give almost as good protection as a garden shelter, and is the method most householders are likely to adopt. The home handyman can often do the necessary work of preparing a refuge room with materials found in his house and garden.

The professional Institutions of Architects, Engineers and Surveyors represented on the Building Technical Advisory Committee have arranged a scheme for providing inexpensive advice for the use of householders in a number of areas. For a fee of half a guinea, a consultant appointed by one of the professional Institutions will inspect your house in these areas and give you a written report stating the best place in which to shelter and describing ways within your means by which your protection can be improved. A list of the Institutions concerned and the addresses from which further information can be obtained will be found at the end of this pamphlet.

The Shelter

The simplest kind of garden shelter is an open trench which will give you complete protection against bomb splinters and very good protection against blast. Covering it over with earth will improve the protection against blast and also keep out falling splinters of anti-aircraft shells. A trench shelter needs materials such as timber and corrugated iron to hold up the earth covering and also, in most soils, to prevent the sides of the trench falling in. Suitable materials are not easy to get at present, though you may find them in your garden or outhouses.

Several kinds of sectional shelters are also marketed that are designed to be put together in a garden trench and to hold up the earth at the sides and overhead. Most of them are made of concrete. Alternatively you can have built on the ground surface, or partly sunk below it, a brickwork or concrete shelter, usually called a "surface-shelter." This can give as much protection as one below the ground, and will be necessary where the ground is too waterlogged to allow deep digging.

Many persons, however, would prefer not to leave their houses, especially at night or in cold, wet weather, and would like a refuge room

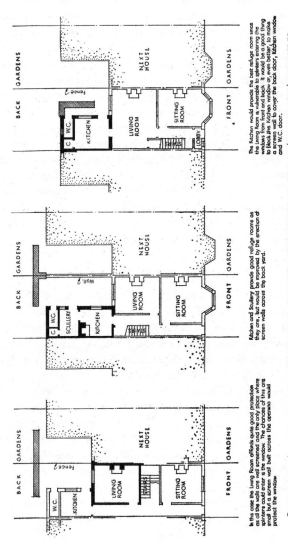

In this case the Living Room affords quite good protection as all the walls are well screened and the only place where splinters could enter is the window. The chances of this are small but a screen wall built across the opening would protect the window.

Kitchen and Scullery provide good refuge rooms as they are, but could be improved by the erection of screen walls across the back yard.

The Kitchen would provide the best refuge room since the Living Room is vulnerable to splinters entering the windows from front and back. It would be a good thing to block the Kitchen window or, even better, to make a screen wall to cover the back door, Kitchen window and W.C. door.

ILLUSTRATION I.—PLANS OF TYPICAL HOUSES SHOWING THE BEST ROOMS IN WHICH TO SHELTER (REFUGE ROOMS) AND HOW TO IMPROVE THEIR NATURAL PROTECTION.

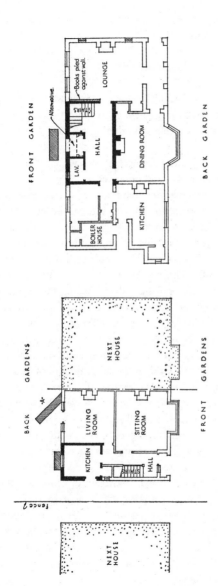

The Kitchen affords good protection, the door is screened by the next house and the window is small and can be readily protected. The two thin inside walls are well protected except from a chance splinter coming through the Living Room window. This window can be also screened as shown at 'A' then almost complete protection would be obtained.

In this case the Hall provides a good refuge room. The front door has to be blocked either by a screen wall outside or by screen wall in the Lobby. The Lavatory window is high and may be blocked but it left open would not constitute a danger to people sitting down. It is desirable to block the two Lounge windows facing the Hall door if they are low.

[ILLUSTRATION I (CONTD.)]

81

in the house. In some cases a surface shelter can be built against a house with a door opening from it.

The Refuge Room

A refuge room below ground-level is best because it gives natural protection against bomb splinters. Very good protection can, however, be obtained above ground where the refuge room is well enclosed by brick or stone walls.

Illustration 1 shows plans of typical houses which illustrate how refuge rooms should be chosen and improved.

The room chosen should be one that is as well protected as possible by surrounding walls of brick, stone or concrete, including those of the house next door and garden walls, the object being to provide as much protection as possible against flying bomb splinters, and that even 9 inches of it will stop a great many. The whole of this protection need not be found in the walls within a distance of about 30 feet from the refuge room. Make certain that the walls enclosing the refuge are of solid brickwork or stonework and not of timber framing covered with stucco or weather-boarding, as these provide no protection.

A small or narrow room is to be preferred, because, in the event of part of the house collapsing from a very near explosion, the roof or ceiling over it will be more capable of resisting the fall of debris, such as loose slates or tiles, than a roof of wide span. Of course, if you can get material and labour for propping up the ceiling over the refuge room, it is not so important to choose a small and narrow room.

As a general rule it is desirable to avoid rooms with large windows; bay windows in particular will require large amounts of material to block them in order to keep out blast and splinters.

In the typical suburban house, the kitchen or scullery will often, though not always, be found to be the most suitable, particularly if the door faces either the next house or a garden wall. A ground floor room should generally be chosen in preference to one on an upper floor as it provides greater overhead protection against falling shell splinters or machine-gun fire. Also bomb splinters may strike upwards through window openings and floors.

If you live in the upper storey of a house which has been converted into flats it will be necessary to come to some arrangement with the other occupants, so that common protection can be secured for all. People in the ground floor or basement might give up space in an entrance hall or the like, and the others might provide material and labour for blocking up a window where necessary. Perhaps a common staircase could be adapted for use as a refuge by all.

A coal cellar under the pavement or under a yard at the back of a house will make a very good shelter just as it is, but you should see, if possible, that there is an emergency exit. This can be provided by enlarging the coal chute as shown in Illustration 2. If you live in a terrace it may be possible to arrange with your neighbour to make a crawl hole between your cellars.

Illustration 2.—An enlarged coal chute protected from debris can be arranged as an emergency exit from cellars.

Protection of Windows and Doors of Refuge Rooms

Windows and doors of refuge rooms which are not shielded by another house or solid wall within a short distance must be protected against bombs. This protection can be obtained by blocking the openings or by erecting a brick or earth wall outside. The latter is known

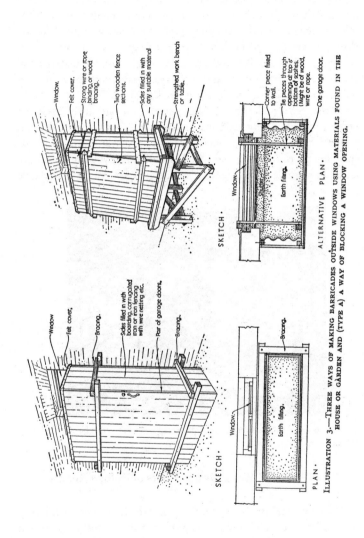

Window.

Felt cover.

Strong wire or rope binding, or wood bracing.

Two wooden fence sections.

Sides filled in with any suitable material

Strengthed work bench or table.

SKETCH.

Corner piece fixed to wall.

Window.

Shutter.

Earth filling.

Tie pieces through openings at top & bottom of sashes. (Might be of wood, wire or rope.

One garage door.

ALTERNATIVE PLAN.

Window.

Felt cover.

Bracing.

Sides filled in with boarding, corrugated iron or iron fencing with wire netting etc.

Pair of garage doors.

Bracing.

SKETCH.

Window.

Bracing.

Earth filling.

PLAN.

ILLUSTRATION 3.—THREE WAYS OF MAKING BARRICADES OUTSIDE WINDOWS USING MATERIALS FOUND IN THE HOUSE OR GARDEN AND (TYPE A) A WAY OF BLOCKING A WINDOW OPENING.

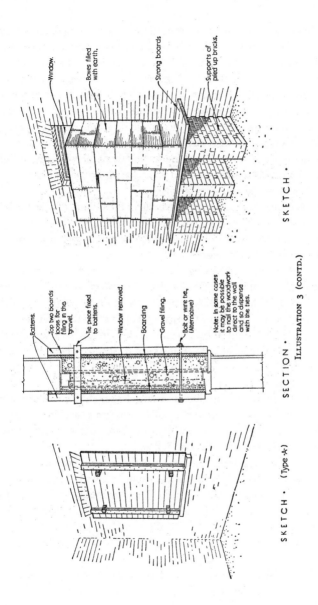

Window.

Boxes filled with earth.

Strong boards

Supports of piled up bricks.

SKETCH.

ILLUSTRATION 3 (CONTD.)

Battens.

Top two boards loose for filling in the gravel.

Tie piece fixed to battens.

Window removed.

Boarding

Gravel filling.

Bolt or wire tie, (Alternative)

Note: In some cases it may be possible to nail the woodwork direct to the wall and so dispense with the ties.

SECTION.

SKETCH. (Type 'A')

85

as a "barricade." In either case the protection should be raised to a height of at least 6 ft. above the floor of the room, so that you can walk about without danger from splinters. Where a window is blocked up to a height of 6 ft. above floor level this will usually leave a small area of window at the top which can be used to admit light and air at normal times. If you find it too expensive to provide protection up to 6 feet high, protection up to 3 feet 6 inches will do if you are prepared to sit on the floor during raids. An inside screen (as described on page 96) should be fitted to the refuge room window. This will prevent light from showing in a black-out, and if the glass is broken will stop flying pieces of glass and also keep out gas.

If you can get the help of somebody in the building trade, the best plan is, of course, to build up the window opening with brickwork. Old bricks will serve just as well as new ones; the builder will probably have some. There is no shortage of bricks.

A simple way of blocking the window is shown in Illustration 3, type A. Whilst this does not give absolute protection it will stop most splinters. It is done by nailing up stout boards on either side of the window opening and filling the space between them with shingle, earth or sand. It will usually be best to remove the window, or at any rate the glass, before doing this. Thick stacks of books form good protection against flying bomb splinters, and Illustration 4 shows two ways of stacking them.

Some ways of making window barricades are shown in Illustrations 3 and 6, and of door barricades, usually called "traverses," in Illustration 5. Methods of barricading the windows of basement or semi-basement rooms are shown in Illustrations 7, 8 and 9.

Loose gravel or shingle, 2 feet thick, or 30 inches of earth or sand, will give complete protection against splinters, and is equivalent to a solid brick wall 13½ inches thick. These materials should be held between boarding, corrugated iron or some form of revetment, as in Illustration 3. Timber may be difficult to get and can be economised by using wire netting or split chestnut fencing between timber uprights spaced not more than 1 foot 6 inches apart. In some cases one or two old doors may be removed and used to contain the earth or gravel walls as shown in Illustration 6.

Illustration 4.—A stout book-case, stuffed tightly with old books, protects one window. Or a table can be used with books 2 ft. 6 in. thick piled on it. If the books are loose, rope them down firmly.

Timber or other outside framing should be firmly tied together through the earth wall to prevent bulging. For this, cross pieces of wood may be nailed on, or lengths of wire used. The earth gravel need not be rammed tightly. There is, of course, no objection to providing earth or gravel walls thicker than is specified above; the aim should be to make the window barricade give at least as much protection as the walls of the house. Crazy paving slabs make an excellent material for building walls or filling barricades.

In blocking windows and building barricades you should take care to avoid making the house damp or starting dry rot in the woodwork of the house. Barricades should either be built a few inches away from the walls or be insulated from them by layers of tarred building paper or waterproofed felt. It is as well to cover the tops of barricades with building paper or slates in cement mortar to keep them from becoming

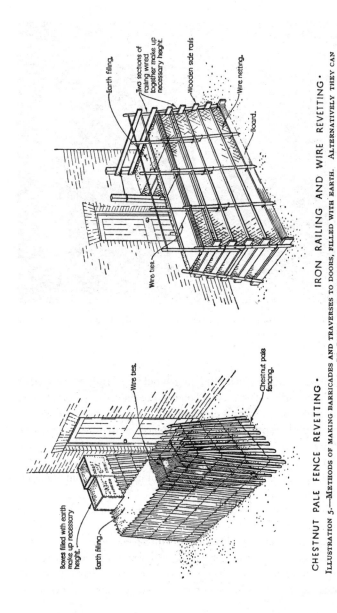

CHESTNUT PALE FENCE REVETTING·   IRON RAILING AND WIRE REVETTING·

Boxes filled with earth make up necessary height.

Wire ties.

Chestnut pals fencing.

Earth filling.

Earth filling.

Two sections of railing wired together make up necessary height.

Wooden side rails

Wire netting.

Board.

Wire ties.

ILLUSTRATION 5.—METHODS OF MAKING BARRICADES AND TRAVERSES TO DOORS, FILLED WITH EARTH. ALTERNATIVELY THEY CAN BE BUILT OF BRICKWORK.

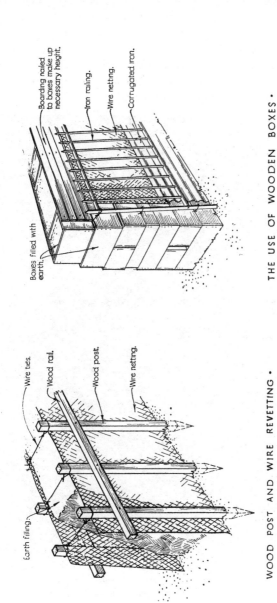

WOOD POST AND WIRE REVETTING •   THE USE OF WOODEN BOXES •

Wire ties.

Wood rail.

Wood post.

Wire netting.

Earth filling

Boarding nailed to boxes make up necessary height.

Iron railing.

Wire netting.

Corrugated iron.

Boxes filled with earth.

ILLUSTRATION 5 (CONTD.)

89

soaked by rain. Also be careful to keep free from obstruction the wall gratings that ventilate the spaces under wooden floors. If you want to gas-proof your refuge room make arrangements to block these gratings only when air-raiding appears imminent.

Illustration 6.—Protecting a refuge room against bomb splinters. The window has an old door across the window, stoutly fastened by wire to a second door inside the window. The man is filling the space between the doors with gravel. The glass above is covered all over with an anti-splintering treatment.

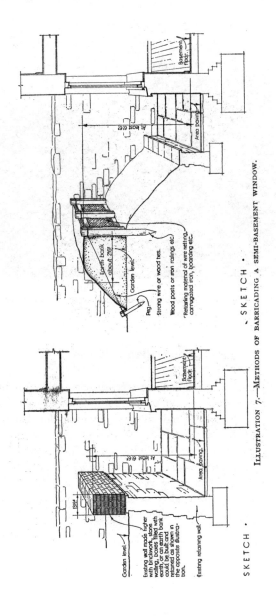

- SKETCH -

- SKETCH -

ILLUSTRATION 7.—METHODS OF BARRICADING A SEMI-BASEMENT WINDOW.

91

Illustration 8.—Piling up earth against a wooden support to form a barricade in front of a semi-basement window.

Protection of Glass in Windows

Even if only a few buildings are seriously damaged by bombing, it is certain that many more will have windows broken by blast. Apart from rooms with broken windows being very uncomfortable, there is the serious danger that people in refuge rooms will be cut by flying pieces of glass when a bomb explodes near by. There are three ways (described in detail below) of overcoming this. These are:—

(1) Paste a suitable covering over the glass.

(2) Cover the whole window inside with wire netting.

(3) Fit inside the window a light-weight screen.

Illustration 9.—Another idea for protecting a window, using two old doors and some old paint cans to support the earth. The old linoleum is to protect the earth from soaking and washing away the rain.

First Method

You should realise that nothing you can stick on to glass will prevent it being broken, nor will even increase its chance of remaining unbroken when a bomb explodes near by. But a good covering, properly stuck on, will prevent glass flying in small dangerous pieces and may even hold a badly cracked and bulged pane in place enough to keep out the weather for a time. Coverings of this kind are suitable where curtains and blinds are used for blackout.

The material chosen should be tough or one that will stretch considerably without breaking, and it must of course stick tightly to the glass. Both the material and the adhesive should keep their nature for a reasonably long time on the window. If they become brittle or peel off they will be useless.

The following notes will serve as a guide to the various materials you can use. All materials should be put on the inside of the window, which should be thoroughly cleaned beforehand.

(*a*) *Paper or Cardboard.*—Where the loss of light does not matter, sheets of strong wrapping paper or cardboard can be pasted over the glass. The thicker and tougher the paper, the better; if possible, it should be one containing cloth fibre. Thin brown paper applied in strips is not very effective.

It is important that the adhesive should not become brittle on drying. Adhesives such as gum, flour paste, or paperhangers' paste are suitable if a little glycerine is added or, failing glycerine, treacle.

For fixing cardboard, the adhesive should be made rather stronger than for paper, and it is as well to damp the cardboard before applying the paste. Flexible glues can also be used.

Sodium Silicate ("waterglass") should not be used as an adhesive for any material as it is liable to damage the surface of the glass.

(*b*) *Textile Materials.*—Cotton, linen, sisal or other light-coloured cloth in the form of netting or sheeting may be applied all over the glass, using one of the adhesives mentioned in (*a*) above.

More daylight, though rather less effective protection, will be obtained by applying cloth materials in strips. Insulation tape and sticky cloth tape of the kind used for wrapping tennis racquet handles are examples of this. These will stick to the glass better if they are pressed on with a warm iron. The strips should preferably be not less than 1½ inches wide, and should be put on to form spaces not more than 6 inches each way.

(*c*) *Transparent Wrapping Films.*—Special transparent films similar to those sold for wrapping cigarette packets, chocolate boxes, etc., but rather thicker, can be bought. These give good protection and do not cut off light as much as paper or textiles. Some films can be obtained strengthened with a light fabric netting.

Films are sold under several trade names, and sometimes have a suitable adhesive sold with them. Some are supplied in rolls ready-coated with a tacky adhesive, and these can be put on to the glass in strips.

Most of the films now being sold belong to one or other of the following types, which can be easily distinguished by the burning tests described below.

(1) *Cellulose nitrate film*, commonly called "celluloid." This is highly inflammable and for this reason should not be used on windows. It flames fiercely when set on fire.

(2) *Cellulose film.*—This burns quietly like newspaper when set on fire. There are two types; the "coated" or moisture-proofed kind, should not be used. You can tell the "uncoated" by wetting it with the tongue when it will curl and soften slightly, whereas the "coated" will not.

Suitable adhesives are a good clear gum, or gum Arabic or gelatine dissolved in hot water. These should have one part in six of glycerine or treacle added. Do not try to put the adhesive on to the film itself, but smear it on the glass and then press the dry film into place quickly. It is best to use a small hand roller. If the panes are large it will be easier to put on an all-over coating in strips, side by side, rather than in once piece. It does not matter if the film wrinkles provided most of it sticks firmly when dry. It is possible to make cellulose film stick smoothly and evenly by wetting it with water only, but this should on no account be done since the coating so applied gives little or no protection. After the cellulose film has dried it is useful to apply a coat of clear varnish or cellulose lacquer. This waterproofs the film and will help to prevent it peeling off if the windows get steamy.

(3) *Cellulose acetate film.*—This does not readily take fire, and in burning it melts and drops. Gum is not a suitable adhesive. If no special adhesive is recommended by the maker, a mixture of nine parts of treacle to one of warm water may be used and the edges stuck down with adhesive tape.

(*d*) *Liquid Coatings.*—Liquid preparations for painting on the glass are now being sold under various trade names as "anti-shatter" treatments. When dry they usually give a clear coating which sticks to the glass, but some are sold coloured for blackout purposes. The makers issue instructions for putting on their own materials.

Not all of these give the desired protection, and at best they usually do not last long. They tend to become brittle, and lose their anti-splintering effect, and it is not always possible to see they have done so. It is safest, therefore, to renew the coating every two or three months.

Second Method

Wire netting of mesh not bigger than ½ inch will stop flying glass. It should be firmly fixed on the inside of the window. It may be nailed to the window frame, but this will make the window difficult to clean or open. A better way is to fix it to a detachable wooden frame made to fit the window opening. Wire netting of course gives no protection against weather when the glass is broken, nor does it help in blacking out.

Third Method

A light-weight screen fixed over the window opening inside has four uses. When the window is broken it will stop flying pieces of glass, it will keep out the weather and, if properly fitted, it will keep out gas and it also acts as blackout. A screen is the best method of protecting a refuge room window. Pasting a covering on the glass as well is not necessary, but makes a better job of protection.

The screen is made of a light sheet material which is nailed to a light wooden frame. Materials such as the following are suitable:—

> Plywood, Building Board, Thick Cardboard, Corrugated Fibre Board, Thin Tinned Sheets, Roofing Felts, Linoleum, Plaster Board.

Some of these materials, which are very stiff (such as Building Board), can be used for small windows without a frame. Those which are not themselves waterproof can be made reasonably rainproof with a coat of paint. Screens of paper or cloth will not stop flying pieces of glass.

Illustration 10 shows some typical methods of framing the screens. A screen for a window 6 ft. high by 4 ft. wide can be framed with 1¾ in. x 1 in. wood, and if this is covered with stiff material like building board no cross members will be needed, but if covered with less stiff material such as roofing felt or linoleum one or two cross members should be provided in each direction, partly to strengthen the frame and partly to provide something to nail the sheets to. See details (1), (2), (3) and (4) of Illustration 10.

THE SCREEN COMPLETE

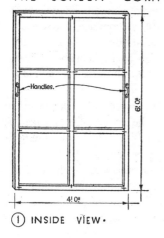

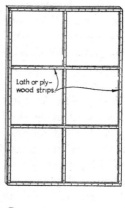

① INSIDE VIEW·

② OUTSIDE VIEW·

SKETCHES OF ALTERNATIVE JOINTS FOR FRAME

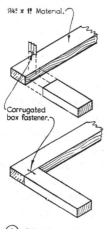

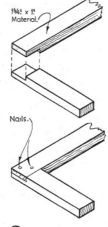

③ BUTT JOINT·

④ HALVED JOINT·

ILLUSTRATION 10.—MAKING LIGHT-WEIGHT SCREENS.

There is nothing to be gained by making the screens extra strong or heavy; the lighter they are the less they are likely to be broken when a bomb explodes. Large windows may need more than one screen.

Strong sheet materials can be nailed direct to the frame, but the thinner materials such as corrugated fibre board should be held between plywood strips or plasterer's laths as shown in details (5) and (6) of Illustration 11.

A strip of rubber, felt, baize, old carpet or other thick fabric may also be tacked on the outside edge of the screen frame to make a tight fit with the window surrounds (detail 7). This will make a tight fit to hold the screen in place, and will keep out gas.

If these screens are screwed to or otherwise firmly fixed in the window openings they will be broken by blast. They should therefore be kept in place by their tight fit or by means of the lightest possible fixings, and they will then fall out undamaged, if subjected to blast, and can be quickly replaced.

A good plan to prevent the screens from falling on the floor when blown out by blast is to hold them at the top by an elastic or rubber cord fixed to the window head. Rings cut from old inner tyre tubes from motor cars will do for this. (Details (9), (10), (11) and (12) of Illustration 11.)

Fire Precautions

This pamphlet does not deal with fire precautions, but you should know how to deal with incendiary bombs if one falls on the house when you are in your refuge or shelter. Also you should take precautions beforehand to prevent fire spreading. You should study carefully Public Information Leaflet No. 5 which advises you to:—

1. Clear your roof spaces and attics of any old "junk" that you have collected there. See that you have nothing there that will easily catch fire and nothing that would prevent you getting at the burning bomb.

2. Make sure that you can easily get into your attic or roof space.

3. Have ready at least four large buckets, a shovel or scoop, preferably with a long handle, and a fair quantity of sand or dry earth. Provide also what appliances you can; if possible, a stirrup handpump

with the special nozzle giving either a jet of water for playing on a fire, or spray for dealing with the bomb itself. Failing this, a garden syringe would be useful, or even old blankets soaked in water.

Taking Cover

And now about taking over.

You have been told at the beginning of this pamphlet what happens when a bomb bursts, and from what you have been told about your own home you will know what it is that gives you the necessary protection against blast and splinters, and this knowledge will be a help to you in taking cover.

Experience in war areas has shown that casualties for the civil population fall to very small numbers when people learn to take cover and avoid exposing themselves in the open to bomb and anti-aircraft splinters, machine-gun bullets and flying glass.

The first thing to remember is that you are safer at home than running into the streets and seeking other shelter when a warning goes, and you will certainly be much more comfortable in your own refuge room or garden shelter.

Almost no shelter is proof against a direct hit from a heavy bomb, but the chances of *your own* house getting a direct hit are very small indeed. Therefore stay at home or if you are not far away when a warning goes, get back quickly to your own home and refuge. On no account look out of the window.

If you are not near home and you are caught in the street or in the open take the best cover you can find.

Remember that bomb splinters do not as a rule fly horizontally; practically all of them fly slightly upwards. Therefore if you are in the open with no cover lie down flat on your face. If there is a ditch get into it, or a low mound or wall get down behind it.

If you are caught in a street go into the nearest public shelter, if there is one and you know where it is. You should make a habit of memorising the situations of public shelters in the places and streets which you frequent.

METHODS OF FIXING SHEET MATERIAL TO FRAME

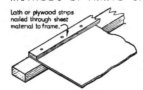

Lath or plywood strips nailed through sheet material to frame.

Sheet material turned up over edge of frame and nailed to

⑤ LATH OR PLYWOOD STRIPS ·

⑥ NAILING DIRECT TO FRAME ·

EDGE FIXING & GASPROOFING

CORRUGATED BOARD SCREENS

⑦ Rubber, felt, baize or similar material tacked to edge of frame.

⑧ Edge of board folded and turned.

TURNBUTTON FIXING

ELASTIC BAND SUSPENSION

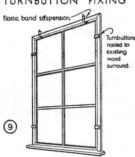

Elastic band suspension.

Turnbuttons nailed to existing wood surround.

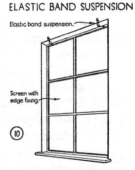

Elastic band suspension.

Screen with edge fixing.

⑨

⑩

SCREEN IN POSITION ·

SCREEN IN POSITION ·

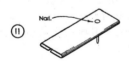

⑪ Nail.

⑫ Frame.

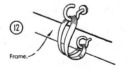

SKETCH OF TIN TURNBUTTON ·

SKETCH OF SUSPENSION HOOK ·

ILLUSTRATION 11.—MAKING LIGHT-WEIGHT SCREENS.
Detail (9) shows a screen held by turnbuttons as in detail (11). Detail (10) shows a screen held by its tight fit in the window opening.

Do not, however, waste time hunting for a public shelter. Go into the most solid-looking building near you, if you can. Inside corridors and passages are safer than rooms with windows, and avoid all places where bomb splinters or flying glass can hit you.

If you cannot get into a building get under an archway or behind a low wall, or even into an area, or lie down flat. Do not, however, lie down in front of a window because glass when broken sometimes flies or falls outwards.

If bombs are bursting near it is useful to keep the mouth open by gripping a piece of wood or rubber tightly between the teeth and to put loosely-packed plugs of cotton wool in the ears. The necessary materials should be obtained and kept in a convenient place where they may be readily found if required.

Always take cover. Never go into the open to watch anti-aircraft fire or aerial battles. They may be terribly fascinating, but it is dangerous.

Another point is this. If you live in a well-built house or have a good refuge, look into the street when the warning goes and see if there is a passer-by wanting shelter and ask him in—you may be "a passer-by" in the next raid.

A.R.P. AT HOME
Hints for Housewives
by
MRS. CRESWICK ATKINSON, R.R.C.
Welfare Adviser to London
Regional Headquarters
Issued by the Ministry of Home Security, 1941

Shelters

Is your shelter clean and always ready for use?

Do you take part in keeping things clean and neat if you use a public or communal shelter?

Try to do your share and feel that you have a certain responsibility for the way in which the shelter is kept.

Anderson Shelters

If you have an Anderson shelter in your garden, is the earth covering thick enough?

Is the back wall covered with earth as well as the top and sides?

The earth covering should be 15 inches deep on the top, 30 inches thick at the sides, and 30 inches deep at the back. It is the **earth covering** which **protects**, not the steel walls.

Is the entrance protected by a wall, barricade, or the wall of a house not more than 15 feet away from it?

This protection can be made of bricks or of earth raised to a height of at least 3 feet 6 inches, and it should be 13 inches thick if brick, 30 inches thick if earth.

Do go and look at your shelter and see whether the earth really is thick enough—if it is not, remedy matters now—you may be thankful some day.

Have you padded the top of the entrance so that heads will not suffer when getting inside in a hurry?

Is your Anderson shelter dry?

If the earth covering is not thick enough, and not properly rammed down, you may have temporary flooding from surface water.

Leakage can often be cured by taking off the top part of the earth covering and replacing it (using more earth if necessary) in layers of 4 inches or 5 inches, ramming each layer well down, or treading it down, before putting on the next. Make the side slopes even and beat them with a spade.

If you have any old linoleum it is a good plan to lay it over the surface, and replace the top layers of earth over it.

You should dig channels round the limits of the earth covering to take the surface water away.

Leakage of rain water into the shelter through the top and sides can be stopped by clay puddling. Mix any stiff soil with water to the consistency of dough and plaster all over and round the joists of the shelter, afterwards replacing the earth cover, well rammed down.

If you find that water still leaks in through the joints of the corrugated iron sheets, caulk them from the inside with rope or old rags soaked in heavy oil or tar.

Perhaps surface water is finding its way through the floor. If it is, dig a sump 1 foot deep in one corner of the shelter near the entrance.

The water will drain into it and you can remove it by baling, but keep the hole covered when you are in the shelter.

You can help towards keeping things dry by covering the floor with a layer of bricks with linoleum over them.

It is a wise plan, before you try to get your shelter dry, to ask for advice from your local council. Their experts will know what is the matter and whether the trouble can be cured by your own efforts. If it cannot, they will do the work for you.

Is your shelter draughty?

You can cure this by arranging a screen at the entrance or by hanging curtains in front of the bunks.

Are bunks installed in your shelter? Do you know that four adults and two children can sleep comfortably in a standard Anderson shelter?

You may find it quicker, if you have a handy man about the house, to make bunks for the shelter at home. Consult your local authority. The local council's expert may be able to advise you.

Have you provided lighting in your shelter?

You can get a good light from candle lamps or a night light, but see that no light can be seen from the outside. Don't use oil lamps, they may get upset either by accident or as a result of an explosion nearby. Don't sleep with a light in the shelter, it may make the air foul, and when you are asleep you won't know this is happening.

Before you settle down to sleep, put the light out and air the shelter.

You may not sleep well if you don't do this.

Brick Street Shelters

If a brick street shelter has been allotted to you, have you made the most of it?

Such a shelter can easily be made into a place where you can spend the night hours not only in comfort and security, but under conditions where your health and the health of your family will not suffer.

Have bunks been installed and lighting put in?

Many local authorities will do this or show you how to do it.

You should enquire at your council offices.

Has the shelter been fitted with a door and lock and key?

Ask for this if it has not been done.

Have you painted or colour-washed the walls, and whitewashed the ceiling?

It will appear much more homelike if you can do this. When dealing with the walls use a light colour, such as pale yellow; a dark or bright colour will make the shelter seem smaller.

Do you take a coal, coke, or any other type of brazier into the shelter at night?

Never do this. Such stoves are dangerous, except under a good chimney.

Don't use oil stoves at night either; they too may be a source of danger.

Do you know that anything which burns uses up the oxygen in the air which you breathe?

To prevent danger from bad air your shelter should be kept well ventilated.

Never close up the ventilation openings in the walls. To do so is even worse than sleeping in a room where the windows are shut tight and the chimney, keyhole, etc., blocked up.

Have you thought of a safe way of heating your shelter?

You won't want heat in the summer, but in winter the best way to keep warm is by using a hot-water bottle or a hot brick in your bed.

Another way to obtain heat is to use a "flower-pot stove." You will need two large flower pots and a candle for this.

1. Fix the candle at one side of the hole in the bottom of one of the pots (don't place it **over** the hole), and stand the flower pot on something which will raise it from the ground; three empty cotton reels of the same size do very well.
2. Light the candle and put the second flower pot upside down on the top of the first.
3. If you want to keep a kettle hot, place a metal curtain ring on the top and stand the kettle on it.

This candle stove does not use up enough oxygen to be dangerous, and as the top flower pot warms up, heat will be given off.

Have you covered the floor of your shelter?

Cocoanut matting or rugs are the best sort of covering. Don't use linoleum, damp may result.

Is your shelter damp, and if so have you informed your local authority? You should; they will put it right for you.

To get the walls inside dry after it has been put right you can use an oil stove **during the day**. Take it out at night.

Do you realise how convenient a shelter of this type can be?

Instead of keeping children up late, they can be put to bed in the shelters in good time and are close enough for you to be able to keep an eye on them.

Have you thought of forming your own street shelter "communities"?

You could start a library, children's play groups, handicraft classes, study circles and perhaps start a little choral society or hold "sing-songs."

Ask your local authority whether you may use two disused shelters in the street for this purpose.

You could link up with the Fire Guards, perhaps. You won't need this sort of activity in the summer but when the dark days come you will be glad of something to keep you all cheerful and happy; so make plans **now**.

Are you a member of the W.V.S. Housewives Service?

If you are you could interest other members of the Service in the idea of street shelter "communities," and together could plan what could be done and how it could be done.

Ask your Post Air Raid Warden whether there is any official who could advise you about this, and if there is not consult the W.V.S. Centre Organiser in your district. Ask the Council Offices where she can be found.

Indoor Shelters

If you have or are having a table indoor shelter, do you know where it should be placed in the house?

Such a shelter must be placed on the floor of the basement or cellar, or if you have no basement or cellar, on the ground floor. It must never be used on a floor which has another floor below it.

Have you thought of covering it with a tablecloth or sheet before settling down for the night?

A covering of this kind may serve to protect you somewhat from dust if your house is damaged as a result of high explosive.

There is a Ministry of Home Security booklet "Shelter at Home," price 3d. from any newsagent, which tells you all about these things, including how to make a refuge room.

Brick or Concrete Garden Shelters

Have you done all you can to make your shelter comfortable?

Almost all the suggestions made for the Brick Street Shelters apply equally well to a garden shelter of this type.

Windows

Have you protected your window glass against splintering if you still have any glass to protect?

You should do this and as soon as possible. More injuries are still caused in this way than in any other.

Do you know how to do it?

1. Cut pieces of net or old lace curtains slightly larger than the pane to be covered.
2. Paste these pieces on to the glass so that there is an overlap on to the frame.

A good paste can be made in this way:—

Take 2 level tablespoonfuls of flour, plain or self-raising, and 3 tablespoonfuls of cold water. Mix the flour and water into a smooth paste. Stir in a piece of washing-soda the size of an almond. Add ½ pint of boiling water and stir briskly. Cook in a double saucepan for ten minutes and use hot.

3. Wet the material thoroughly with the paste.
4. Spread it on to the pane to be covered.
5. Work it on with a clean brush.

If you prefer it, there are several types of window varnish which you can use instead.

Are you learning to curb your curiosity? For instance, would you still go to the window or into the street if you heard gunfire?

Never do this. Keep away from the windows; this means, placing yourself where you cannot see out.

Don't sit or lie underneath or in front of a window which has glass in it.

If you remember this, and the glass does shatter, it will not injure you, and if you have protected it, it will not splinter.

Have you ever had to clean up a room into which glass has shattered?

If you have you will know that you should wear thick gloves if you can, and that you will have to watch out for splinters, especially if you have not been wise enough to protect your glass.

Splinters penetrate to the most unlikely places, and they can ruin furniture and upholstery. Examine all exposed food **with the greatest care** for tiny particles of glass. **Take no chances.**

Have you thought of protecting your furniture?

It is a wise plan to cover it all at night with dust sheets, old quilts, tablecloths, curtains, etc. This may prevent deep scratches on the furniture if the house is damaged by enemy action and will help to keep upholstery clean if dust or soot falls.

Shelter Preparations

Before you go to Shelter

Have you packed a bag with a complete change of clothing, and have you left it with a friend who lives some streets away from you or in another part of the town?

Nothing is more embarrassing or annoying than to be left without clothes, if you have to leave your home.

Where do you keep your valuables and the papers which you do not wish to lose and which cannot be easily replaced?

Valuables and such papers as insurance policies, deeds, etc., should be put away in a safe place. If you cannot do this they should be taken to shelter with you.

Do you keep or carry large sums of money with you?

Don't do this, it is most unwise. The best thing to do is to put all spare money into National Savings. It will be safe there and you can easily get it if you need it.

What precautions do you take before you leave the house?

Draw back all curtains or raise blinds in upper rooms, so that if a fire is started it can be readily seen from the outside.

Do you turn off all gas taps, and also turn off the gas at the main before leaving the house?

Do this and do not forget also to turn off all pilot jets, and your electricity at the main.

Do you leave fires burning in the house?

Try not to do this, damp them down before you go. Salt will help to put them out.

Do you lock the doors of your house or flat when you leave?

Don't do this, or, if you do, see that some responsible person has the key. Put a notice on your door to say where the keys are.

Do you wrap up warmly if you have to go outside to shelter?

You should—remember that although it may be quite warm when

you go, it may be cold when you leave in the early morning. You may need, too, to get up during the night and the warm wraps may prove a blessing.

What you should take with you to shelter

Do you know the things which you should have with you?

Identity card, rent book, building society book, record of instalment payments, ration card.

Gas Mask.

Shaded torch (if "black-out" is early).

If the weather is cold, a hot-water bottle or hot bricks which you have heated in a hot oven or in front of the fire for two hours, wrapped up in your rugs or bedding to keep them warm.

Slippers and clean stockings or socks—you may get your feet wet on the way to shelter and there is no more sure way of catching cold than by sitting with wet feet.

Something to do (knitting, etc.), something to read.

Toilet soap, towel, toilet paper, something to drink out of, if you use a public shelter.

Anything else which you have found by experience that you need.

While You Are In Shelter

If you use a public shelter, do you do your best to help the Shelter Warden in seeing that rules are obeyed?

Do this—obedience to Wardens may be irksome but may prove more important than you think; it has often resulted in saving life.

Always back up the Shelter Warden—his authority is your protection.

Do you know that Wardens have been given authority to act in certain cases?

They have authority to enforce certain of the shelter rules, and the police act in co-operation with them.

Have you found out whether you can give any help in the shelter?

People may be needed to help with the canteen, to act as librarians, to help in the organisation of occupation for the shelterers.

You may be able to do some of these things.

Do you do all you can to get and to keep a happy spirit amongst all who shelter with you?

A good aspect of public shelters is the wonderful "family" feeling which has grown up amongst shelterers.

Your bed

Do you know the best form of bedding for shelter use?

It is a sleeping-bag, easy to make either from the blankets you already have or from pieces of old material you have by you.

Do you know how to make one?

1. Take a blanket or rug (or pieces of material joined together) about 7 feet long and 6 feet 6 inches wide.
2. Fold the two sides of the blanket towards the centre.
3. Before you start sewing it together sew on pieces of tape about 6 inches long at each bottom corner. These pieces of tape are to tie up with similar pieces sewn on the loose inside sheet or blanket which you will use inside the bag.
4. Now sew across the bottom of the folded blanket, leaving the tapes outside as this is the wrong side of your sleeping-bag.
5. Sew up the centre and edges where the edges of the folded blanket meet to within 2 feet of the top.
6. Sew tapes about 6 inches long opposite to each other on these open edges, so that they can be tied together when you are inside the bag.
7. Sew tapes on to the folded sheet or blanket which you are going to use inside.
8. Arrange this lining sheet or blanket **over** the bag and tie up the tapes.
9. Now turn the whole thing inside out and your bag is ready for use with its loose lining in place.

The sleeping-bag should be ironed inside and out every month.

Do you know that when you are not sleeping on a thick mattress you need as much covering **under** you as **over** you?

You can use a thick layer of newspaper or brown paper on your bunk. Paper is draught-proof and does not conduct heat away.

If you prefer to use loose bedding, have you thought of making a "sleeping tidy"?

This consists of a piece of thin brightly coloured or striped cotton material sufficiently large to cover your bunk. Sew tapes on the bottom corners long enough to tie on to the bunk frame, and longer pieces at the top corners which you can tie on to the bunk frame when you have settled down.

This will keep your bedding cosily in place and will prevent it from falling off your bunk during the night.

In addition "sleeping tidies" help to keep a shelter neat and give a bright and pleasant aspect.

Do you take your bedding out of the shelter every day?

Bedding should be aired daily. You realise the importance of this in your home; it is still more important where a shelter is concerned.

Daily airing will help to keep bedding sweet and fresh and will help to get rid of dampness.

In the driest of shelters bedding will get damp owing to humidity during the night, and many ills may result from sleeping in damp bedclothes.

Do you know that ironing helps to keep bedding fresh and dry?

Try to iron your bedding or sleeping-bag regularly. It will help to keep it dry and clean.

Do you take your washable bedding home once a week to launder?

You should—you would not like to be thought an unpleasant neighbour.

Do you store your bedding with other people's during the day?

Do not do this if you can possibly avoid it.

Infection can be spread in this way and it will mean that your bedding never gets aired.

Air cannot penetrate through layer upon layer of material folded tightly, so even if you have to store your bedding in this way, be sure you take it home once a week for a thorough airing.

If you are allowed to leave your bedding in the shelter, and must do so because you cannot take it home daily, do you roll it up into a bundle in the morning?

You should leave it neatly folded, laid out on the bunk, not rolled up.

There will be more chance of air penetrating through it if it is laid out in this way than if it is rolled up.

Never, never, leave your bed unmade, just as you have got out of it—

But if you possibly can, take your bedding home daily for airing, even if the Shelter Warden does tell you that you may leave it in the shelter.

Sleep

Do you snore? Try to lie on your side, not on your back. If you are in the habit of turning on to your back during the night and snoring results, try tying something hard in the middle of your back (a cotton reel); this may prevent you from lying on your back during the night.

Do you toss and turn whilst trying to get to sleep? Try not to do so. It really makes you more wakeful and disturbs others.

Do you go to rest in heavy outer clothing? You will sleep better if you remove heavy outer garments before you settle down for the night. You will need the extra warmth when you get up in the morning.

Children

Do you try to persuade mothers to send their children to the country or to go there with them? Try to do this. The best public shelter in the world is no place for children.

Do you make your children realise that when they are in a public shelter they must take their part in making things happy for everyone?

Trampling over other people's toes or belongings won't help.

Do you put the little ones to rest early?

You should—children need all the sleep you can manage to get for them. That is why it is better to have a shelter of your own. If you go to a public shelter it is unlikely that the little ones will be able to get to sleep as early as they should.

Do you get impatient with other children in the shelter?

Try not to do so, and if you possibly can, join in arranging play groups for them, where they can play quietly under supervision whilst their mothers rest.

How do you dress the children?

They should wear their night clothes **under** their outer garments when they start for shelter. Then when bedtime comes the outer clothing can be taken off and they are all ready for bed. So often children are put to rest in a shelter without any change being made in their clothing. This is a mistake. It is unhealthy to wear the same clothes day and night; underwear needs airing after daytime wear. Besides shelters become warmer during the night and it is bad for children to become overheated whilst they sleep.

Do you know that ordinary rules for the care of children are more important now than ever?

A ten or fifteen minutes' rest before and after meals. Plenty of fresh air. Keep them out of doors as much as you can during the day. Regular meals—plenty of drinks between meals. Plenty of milk. Nothing indigestible or exciting at the last meal at night. At this last meal you should avoid giving them such things as cheese, pastry, sausages, strong tea and fried foods.

Do you encourage the little ones to say their prayers even in shelter?

You should. A child gains a great sense of security if it feels that someone is caring for it who is even greater than Mummy or Daddy.

Do you teach your children their name and address as soon as they can talk?

This is very important, because if they become separated from you they will be able to say who they are and where they live.

Do you put a label with the child's name and address on it on to each of your children under ten years of age? You should do this.

Have you taught your children not to touch anything strange which they find lying in street or garden after an air raid? And do you know this yourself?

Anything of the kind should be reported to your Warden or the police at once. It may be dangerous to touch things you do not understand.

If you are caught in the open during a raid

Have you found out which is the nearest public shelter to your shopping centre? If you do not know, find out to-day. You never know when you may need this knowledge.

Are you diffident about taking shelter when the enemy are overhead?

You need not be—discretion is the better part of valour.

Do you know what to do if you need to take shelter when in the country?

Get behind a low wall if there is one handy, or into a ditch, and lie flat, your head in your arms protecting your face.

Do you know what to do if an enemy plane turns machine-guns on you?

Do not run away from the plane. Throw yourself down on your face at once. If you **have** to run, run **towards** the plane not **from** it.

Incendiary Bombs

Have you cleared your attic or top floor of anything which could catch fire easily?

Incendiary bombs will penetrate through slate roof but they will be stopped by the first boarded floor they strike. They can be controlled if dealt with speedily. If you live on the top floor, try not to have inflammable materials lying about.

Have you linked up with the Fire Guards?

You should do so if you possibly can.

Incendiary bombs in the house

Do you keep any equipment for dealing with these bombs in your house? In your attic, on the top floor and downstairs? Receptacles containing water should be on the upper floor and on the ground floor.

Have you got a stirrup pump? You should get one if you possibly can, for a stirrup pump is by far the best way of dealing with incendiary bombs. It is wonderful what it can do.

Do you think that dealing with incendiary bombs is rather fun? It is not wise to treat them with too little respect, because some of these bombs have a small explosive charge in them. It is not in all of them, but caution is necessary—your own particular bomb might be one of them. Ask your Warden for further information on this point.

If you heard the Wardens blowing short sharp blasts on their whistles would you know it meant that incendiary bombs were falling?

When you heard the whistles would you rush into the street?

Don't do this—look first to see if any have fallen through your own roof. You can leave the ones outside for a few minutes, unless they are near something which may catch fire easily.

Even then it is best to search your own house before tackling those outside.

If you found a bomb of this kind in your house, would you try to call the Fire Brigade?

Don't do this straight away. Try to fight the fire yourself first. Remember that yours is probably only one of a number of fires.

Do you know how to set about finding the bomb and dealing with it?

Keep your head and mind how you open doors. The door of a room in which a bomb is burning should be opened with care since the hot gases will have raised the atmospherical pressure in the room. The door will not be so easy to open as in normal circumstances, and when it does open the hot gases and smoke may rush out. In particular, the head should be kept well behind the door. If a door opens towards you, put your foot about three inches away from the opening edge, so that the opening door will be checked and not fly open exposing you to smoke and flames.

Keep behind the door when you are opening it so that it protects you.

Do you know how to use a stirrup pump?

You need three people to work it.

No. 1 to manage the nozzle, which is made so that by pressing a switch down or up, either a spray or a jet of water can be used.

No. 2 to do the pumping—it is fairly hard work.

No. 3 to fetch water as needed, and relieve either No. 1 or No. 2.

When you find the fire don't lose your head.

Get hold of the stirrup pump nozzle and crawl into the room.

Keep your head near the floor, smoke is less dense there.

Take cover behind a chair—sofa—anything which will protect you, and drop right down on your tummy.

Perhaps you will not be able to see at once where the bomb is.

Never mind—don't get fussed—turn on the spray until you do know where it is, then you will not play the "jet" on it by mistake.

Could you recognise the bomb?

You will know it by its white glare.

If you found that it had set fire to something, the curtains for instance, would you lose your head and forget all you had learnt?

Keep calm and remember these instructions:—

Change to "jet" and damp down the fires caused by the bomb first.

But don't leave the bomb entirely, if you do it will cause more fires.

As soon as you have got the flames sufficiently under control not to spread, turn your attention to the bomb.

Do you remember what to do for the bomb?

"Spray" for the bomb, **"Jet"** for the fires.

If you use the "jet" on the bomb you may spread the fire by scattering the molten material about the room.

What would you do when the fire was safely out and the bomb also?

Look into the room below to see if all is safe there too, because these bombs can burn through floor boards and some of the fire-causing substances may have fallen through.

Do you think that using sand indoors is as good as using a stirrup pump?

It is not. It is only the next best thing.

These bombs go on burning when smothered with sand, and fires have been caused because people didn't know this.

If you must use sand, do you know how to do it?

Drop a partly filled sandbag on to the bomb, and when you have controlled it, scoop it up and put it into a bucket and take it out of doors to a place where it can do no harm. Remember, if you leave it to burn out in the bucket it will burn right through it.

But you will need water to put out the fires the bomb has caused.

Will you remember these five points?
1. Keep your head.
2. Protect yourself.
3. A stirrup pump is the best way to deal with incendiary bombs; use **"spray"** not **"jet"** for the bomb.
4. These bombs go on burning under sand.
5. If you lose your head and leave an incendiary bomb to do its worst, you will probably lose your own home and endanger the home of others.

Incendiary bombs in the street

Do you know how to deal with incendiary bombs in the street?

The sandbags placed at lamp-posts and in doorways are for your use.

If the bomb has fallen where it can do no harm let it burn for a few minutes; if it is in a dangerous place tackle it at once.

Do you know how to do this?

Pick up a sandbag—carry it over your shoulder.

As you approach the bomb, shift your sandbag so that you are hugging it and shielding your face with it.

Place it on the bomb—**don't throw it—then run.**

Don't wait to see what happens next.

Do you keep your fire-fighting equipment in order and ready for use?

Buckets filled—hose clean and coiled up—axe in its place.

If you have just dealt with one shower of incendiary bombs, get your equipment ready again immediately. You cannot tell when another shower may come, so always be ready.

What You Should Know About Gas

Do you believe stories of new and dreadful gases which the enemy are preparing?

Do not believe stories like this, they are not true; we know all about the gases which they might use against us.

Are you frightened that the enemy may use gas?

He may do so but there is no need to be frightened if you do the right thing **now** and when the time comes.

If you learn what to do **now** and **remember it** you will have taken the first steps to make such an attack fail in its object.

Have you bought any Anti-Gas ointment?

Do this at once. Ask your chemist for "No. 2 Anti-Gas ointment," price 6d.

Read the instructions on the jar and carry it always.

This ointment protects you against the effects of liquid blister gas. But you must apply it quickly if it is to be fully effective.

What You Should Do Now

Gas Masks

Do you and your family **always** take your gas masks with you wherever you go?

No risk is worth while where gas is concerned.

Do you keep your mask beside you even when you go to bed?

Do you practise wearing your mask once a week?

You should practise regularly and see that your family do so too, even the small children.

Using gas masks in this way will make no difference to them.

They will still protect against gas for as long as they are needed to do so, and the civilian mask is just as effective as those used by members of the Services and the Civil Defence Force.

Have you treated the talc window through which you see, to prevent it from becoming blurred?

Once a week and after each time you have used the mask, dip a finger in water and rub it on a piece of toilet soap. Then smear the soapy finger over the inside surface of the eyepiece, leaving an even thin film of soap all over it.

This film will last a week if you do not use the mask during that time.

Have you asked your Air Raid Warden to test your mask?

Do this if you have not done so. You will then feel sure that it is fitting as it should.

Do you think that your gas mask is a protection against ordinary coal gas?

It is not. Don't forget this. It is made to protect you against war gases.

Children's Masks

Is your child used to wearing its gas mask?

It is most important that it should be.

Do you have trouble in getting your child to wear its mask?

If you do and you have tried in every way you can coax it to wear the mask and have failed, try to get a small playfellow, who does not mind wearing its mask, to come in when you are next trying to get your own child to practise. This very often does the trick for children hate to be made to look ridiculous before their little friends.

Afterwards you must insist on the mask being put on regularly and probably you will find that the child ceases to object after a time.

You must not give way about this—just think of what it may mean to the child.

Another way is to leave the child alone with other children. Children have their own methods of dealing with playfellows who are reluctant to do some special thing, and they will often succeed where you would fail.

There is another way, too, which you could try. Children hate to feel that they are being left out of anything, so get your helpers, the other children, to play some game involving the wearing of gas masks. This dodge will often lure small rebels to unconditional surrender.

If, however, all efforts fail, take your child to the A.R.P. Department of your local authority and explain the situation before the child and ask for a baby helmet to be issued instead of the Micky Mouse Mask. These helmets can often be issued to larger children.

BUT DON'T DO THIS TILL YOU HAVE TRIED ALL OTHER MEANS WITHOUT SUCCESS.

Remember that it will mean perhaps another helmet to pump, and you want to avoid that if possible.

Does your child wear spectacles? And do you know that spectacles must not be worn **under** the mask, but **over** it?

You can make elastic straps to fasten with a hook and eye with tapes at the opposite ends. These tapes can be tied on to the spectacles when wanted.

They could be kept in the gas-mask case, rolled up, hook and eye inwards.

Do you know how to put on a small child's mask?

Have you practised doing it, so that both you and the child know all about it?

Putting on a Child's Gas Mask

If the child wears spectacles, take them off.

Stand behind the child, with the back of its head resting against you, so that its neck is supported.

See that the hook and eye on the harness straps of the mask is undone.

Place your thumbs under the bottom and middle straps on each side.

Lift the mask to the child's face, and catch the chin part under the child's chin.

Then stretch the harness over the head.

See that the mask is straight on the face, the chin fitting snugly into the chin-piece, and no edge turned in. Then fasten the hook and eye.

That is how **you** do it, but do teach the child to do it for itself if possible.

Baby's Anti-Gas Helmet

Have you made it someone's special duty to carry baby's anti-gas helmet when you go to shelter?

Do you keep the helmet clean and in its box?

Is baby used to it?

Putting it to sleep in the helmet for short periods with the skirt of the bag turned up will soon get it accustomed to it. Lots of mothers do this now.

Have you padded the tail-piece well?

You should do this with padding which can be washed when soiled.

Are you sure you know how to put your baby into it?

This is how you should do it:

Open the wire legs of the helmet and click them back.

Lay the helmet down and open the skirt of the bag, turning the top of it back over the window.

See that the wide strap fastened to the turned-up end of the metal tail-piece is out of the way, so that baby will not lie on it.

Pull down the skirt of the bag over baby.

See that both its arms are up inside the bag.

Tie the ends of the drawn tapes together once and draw the tape firmly round the waist, but not so tight as to be uncomfortable.

Finish off by tying the ends in a bow (because a bow is easy to undo).

(To keep out gas, you needn't draw the tape round the waist **tightly**.)

Now bring the supporting piece up between the legs.

Attach the ends of the canvas strap to the buckles on each side of the frame, so as to hold baby firmly in place.

If the helmet has been adjusted to the right length, baby's face should be opposite the middle of the window.

Do you know how to use the hand-pump attached to the helmet?

This is how it is done:

First give at least 12 sharp strokes on the pump to clear the air out of the helmet. Then continue to pump slowly and steadily; 35 or 40 strokes a minute is fast enough to keep out poison gas, and to provide plenty of air for a child even 3 or 4 years of age. If you pump too fast, you will tire yourself out.

You could safely stop pumping for several minutes if necessary, without fear of poison gas entering the helmet in amounts which would be harmful.

If you find that even with these instructions you are not sure how to manage it, let your Air Raid Warden know, and ask him to show you exactly how it should be done.

And don't forget if you have other children to look after, to arrange for a neighbour to come in and help you when an air raid warning sounds.

What you should do in a Gas attack

Do you know what the "gas" warning is?

It is the sound of rattles, like those you used to hear at football matches.

Do you know what to do if they sound?

1. Put on your gas mask at once, even if you are in bed.
2. If you are inside the house, shut all the windows and doors and go upstairs if the building is a tall one.
3. Don't come downstairs or take off your gas mask till you hear the "Gas-Clear" which is the sound of handbells.
4. Do you know how to avoid danger from spray?

If you are outside turn up your collar, put your hands in your pockets, or if you have an umbrella put it up.

Never look upwards. You may get drops of liquid gas in your eyes if you do.

Do you know what to do if you get gassed?

Are you worrying about being caught in the street by a Gas Attack whilst your children are with you?

Don't worry unduly about this. Of course, we can't be certain that raids will take place entirely at night, but we can fairly hope that few of them will be before dusk, and not many after dawn, and during this period between dusk and dawn the babies will be tucked up in their beds, or they should be!

Being indoors gives you extra protection and time to get your little people into their gas masks.

But you will say, "**Suppose** there is a raid during the day when we are out in the street."

Well, remember that you won't be taken unawares; the sirens will sound, and you will be wise to go home at once, if you can.

But if you cannot and you hear gunfire, GET UNDER COVER AT ONCE, whether you hear the gas rattles or not. Then you will have plenty of time to put on masks.

But suppose you can't get under cover before the gas rattles sound?

It is very unlikely that this will happen, but if it did don't stop to put on masks, get the children under cover at once. Go into a shop, any building that is open, or knock on the door of the nearest house and ask to come in.

No one will refuse you.

Now, suppose, in spite of it being extremely improbable, you cannot get under cover with the children.

PUT ON YOUR OWN MASK FIRST and then put on the children's.

You will hate to do this BUT REMEMBER IF YOU GET GASSED, THERE WILL BE NO ONE TO SEE THAT THE CHILDREN ARE SAFE. If you practise putting on your mask, it will hardly delay you in getting on the children's.

If the gas rattles sounded whilst you were at home would you look out of the window to see if anyone was in the street who needed shelter?

Every man and woman should do this; do as you would be done by.

If you saw a mother with children caught by a gas attack in the street, would you help her?

Of course you would.

THE RISK OF A GAS ATTACK IS MUCH LESS IN A COUNTRY AREA, so if your children are safely in the country LEAVE THEM THERE, and if they are not, DO YOUR BEST TO GET THEM INTO THE COUNTRY.

What to do

1. If you breathe in any gas or vapour, put on your mask at once. Better late than never.
2. Keep your mask on even if you feel uncomfortable, and if your child wants to get off its mask, tie its hands down if necessary.
3. If you feel irritation afterwards which does not stop when a little time has passed, go to your Air Raid Warden or ask a member of a First Aid Party what you should do.

Do you know what to do if you see a dark splash on your skin or clothing after or during a gas attack?

It may mean that you have been splashed with liquid blister gas.

This is what you should do.

1. **Dab** the liquid off your skin with your handkerchief or a piece of

soft paper. **Don't wipe it off.** Wiping may spread the liquid. Then burn or bury whatever you have used to do this—it is dangerous.

2. Rub "No. 2 Anti-gas ointment" well into and round the place where the liquid splash has been.

   If you have not got this ointment with you, go to the nearest chemist where you will find a substitute for this and will be told how to use it.

   Anti-gas ointment or the bleach cream which the chemist will show you how to use, must be put on within **five** minutes of your being splashed to be completely effective. Slightly later application may still be in time to reduce the severity of any burn which results.

   If you cannot do this, wash the place as soon as possible with soap, nailbrush and hot water if possible—anyway **wash** it—this may save you a burn.

3. Take off any splashed outer garment **at once** before the liquid has time to soak through to the skin; seconds count.

4. If you are within five minutes of your home, or any place where you know you can get a wash, go there at once and wash yourself with hot water and soap, but before you go inside take off any clothing which you think has been splashed and your shoes also.

   Remember your health matters much more than your feelings, and being modest won't compensate you for nasty burns.

5. If you don't know anywhere to go for this wash which is within five minutes, ask the Air Raid Warden or the police what you should do. They will direct you to a place where you can be cleansed from the gas contamination.

6. If you are at home yourself and someone else is splashed and needs a wash—let him in and help him all you can, but don't touch his splashed clothing, which must be removed before the person enters the house.

Protecting Food against Gas

Do you know how to protect food against gas?

1. Keep all the food you can in cans or air-tight bottles. It will be perfectly safe there.
2. Flour, rice, tea, butter, lard, sugar, etc., should be kept in tins or jars with tightly fitting lids.
3. A good plan is to buy a roll of adhesive tape and put it round the fitting edge of the lids of each jar or tin.

    You can then easily open one when you want it and replace the tape after use.
4. Store all the food you can in cupboards or places where it cannot be splashed with liquid gas.
5. If you think that water or food has been exposed to gas, **do not attempt to try to deal with it yourself.**

    Tell the police or your Air Raid Warden and don't touch it till the local authority experts have examined it and told you it is safe.

Remember this

Blister gas cannot kill you if you wear your gas mask, which protects such vital parts as your lungs and your eyes, and if you do what you have been told to do, you will not develop bad burns on the skin either.

NOTICE

SHELTER
IN UNDERGROUND STATIONS

London Transport asks those who seek shelter in Underground stations to help in maintaining the essential transport facilities which are used by roundly one million passengers daily.

Passengers must be afforded free and uninterrupted use of the platforms and stations and the space used for shelter must therefore be limited. Only the space within the white lines may be used for this purpose. The police have been instructed to enforce this arrangement and those seeking shelter are asked to help them in carrying it out.

Stations and platforms must be vacated in the early morning and before the heavy passenger traffic begins.

Only a limited amount of personal baggage, etc., will be allowed on the premises.

Stations and platforms must be kept free from litter which should be carried away or placed in receptacles provided for that purpose.

LONDON ⬤ TRANSPORT

AFTER THE RAID

Issued by the Ministry of Home Security
London Region Edition December 1940

After the Raid

When you have been in the front line and taken it extra hard the country wants to look after you. For you have suffered in the national interest as well as in your own in the fight against Hitler. If your home is damaged there is a great deal of help ready for you.

You will want to know where this help can be found and whom to ask about it. Here are some hints about how you stand. Remember, in reading them, that conditions are different in different areas and the services may not always be quite the same.

Have Your Plans Ready

You should try to make plans *now* to go and stay with friends or relations living near, but not too near, *in case your house is destroyed*. They should also arrange *now* to come to you if their house is knocked out.

If you have to go and stay with them until you can make more permanent arrangements the Government will pay them a lodging allowance of 5s. per week for each adult and 3s. for each child. Your host should enquire at the Town Hall or Council offices about this.

Your local authority will be setting up an Administrative Centre where your questions can be answered. Look out for posters telling you where this centre is or ask the police or wardens for the address. In the meantime, in case of emergency, find out from the police or wardens where the offices are at which the local authority and the Assistance Board are doing their work for people who have been bombed.

Food and Shelter

If you have not been able to make arrangements with friends or relatives and have *nowhere to sleep and eat* after your house has been destroyed, the best thing to do is to go to an emergency *Rest Centre*. The wardens and policemen will tell you where this is. You will get food and shelter there until you can go home or make other arrangements. You will also find at the Rest Centre an officer whose job it is to help you with your problems. He will tell you how to get *clothes* if you've lost your own, *money*—if you are in need—a new ration book, a new identity card, a new gas mask, etc. Nurses will be there, too, to help with children and anybody who is suffering from shock.

New Homes for the Homeless

A home will be found for you, if you cannot make your own arrangements. If you are still earning your normal wages you may have to pay rent.

If you have had to leave your home and can make arrangements to go and stay with friends or relatives you will be given a free travel voucher, if you cannot get to them without help. Enquire about this at the Rest Centre or Administrative Centre (or if there is no Administrative Centre, at the Town Hall or Council offices).

Tracing Friends and Relatives

To keep in touch with your friends and relatives you should, if you find your own accommodation, send your new address to the Secretary, London Council of Social Services, 7, Bayley Street, Bedford Square, London, W.C.1. Of course, also tell your friends and relatives where you are.

Anyone who is homeless and has been provided with accommodation can be found through the Town Halls, the Council offices and the Citizens' Advice Bureaux, since records are kept. If you have got sons or daughters in the Army, Navy, R.A.F., or the Auxiliary Services, they can find you, too, through their Commanding Officer, wherever you may be—whether you have gone to the country, are in hospital or are with friends. In the London area through the local authorities and through the Citizens' Advice Bureaux the Director of Welfare in the London and Eastern Commands is helping men and women serving in the Forces to maintain contact with their relations who may have had to move.

Furniture and Other Belongings

(1) *If your income is below a certain amount* you can apply to the Assistance Board for:—

(*a*) a grant to replace *essential* furniture* and *essential* household articles;

(*b*) a grant to replace your clothes[†] or those of your family;

(*c*) a grant to replace *tools*[†] essential to your work.

You also have a claim for your other belongings, but these do not come under the Assistance Board's scheme, and you should make your claim on Form V.O.W.1.[‡]

(2) *If your income is above certain limits*, you do not come under the Assistance Board's scheme and should make out a claim for all your belongings on Form V.O.W.1.[§]

The time at which payment can be made for belongings not covered by the Assistance Board's scheme will be settled shortly, when Parliament has passed the War Damage Bill.

(3) If bombing has left you without any *ready cash*, because you have lost your job or cannot get to work to be paid or because you have been hurt, you can apply to the Assistance Board.

Compensation for Damage to Houses

If you *own your house* or hold it on a long lease and it is damaged or destroyed, whatever your income, you should, as soon as possible, make a claim on Form V.O.W.1.[§] The amount of your compensation and the time of paying it will depend on the passing of the War Damage Bill now before Parliament.

---

* The household income must be normally £400 a year or less (*i.e.*, nearly £8 0*s*. 0*d*. per week or less).

† Your income in this case must be normally £250 a year or less (*i.e.*, nearly £5 0*s*. 0*d*. per week or less) or £400 a year or less if you have dependants.

‡ You can get this form at your Town Hall or the office of your Council.

§ You can get this form at your Town Hall or the offices of your Council.

Repairs

If your house can be made fit to live in with a few simple repairs the local authority (apply to the Borough or Council Engineer) will put it right if the landlord is not able to do it. But how quickly the local authority can do this depends on local conditions.

Food

If your gas is cut off, or your kitchen range is out of action, then you may be able to get hot meals at the Londoners' Meals Service restaurants in the London County Council area or at the community kitchens outside that area. A meat dish can be obtained for about 4*d.* to 6*d.* and "afters" for about 2*d.* to 3*d.*, tea for a penny, and children's portions half price. Find out now where these are from the Town Hall, Council offices or the Citizens' Advice Bureau in case of emergency.

The Injured

If you are injured, treatment will be given at First Aid Posts and Hospitals, and:—

(*a*) If your doctor says you are unable to work as a result of a "war injury" you will be eligible to receive an *injury allowance*. Application should be made immediately to the local office of the Assistance Board and you should take with you, or send, a medical certificate from a doctor or a hospital.

(*b*) If you are afterwards found to be suffering from a serious and prolonged disablement, your case will be considered for a disability pension.

(*c*) Widows of workers and Civil Defence Volunteers killed on duty will receive £2 10*s.* 0*d.* a week for ten weeks, after which a widow's pension will become payable. Pensions for orphans and dependent parents are also provided.

Ask at the Post Office for the address of the local branch of the Ministry of Pensions if you want to apply for a pension.

KEEP THIS AND DO WHAT IT TELLS YOU. HELP IS WAITING FOR YOU. THE GOVERNMENT, YOUR FELLOW CITIZENS AND YOUR NEIGHBOURS WILL SEE THAT "FRONT LINE" FIGHTERS ARE LOOKED AFTER!

CHAPTER 5

RADIO & CINEMA

THE DUTY OF THE CITIZEN IN HOME DEFENCE
by General Sir Hugh Elles,
Chief of the Operational Staff of the
Civil Defence Services

Broadcast, Wednesday, 5th June 1940, 9.00 p.m.
(Home Service News)

There has lately been a lot of rumour and speculation, especially in the Eastern counties, on the subject of invasion. A great many questions have been asked; and people are puzzled as to what is the duty of the civilian population in the event of invasion.

Now, the danger of invasion is no new one. The Prime Minister, indeed, reminded us yesterday that about 140 years ago, Napoleon gathered a very large army at Boulogne and made immense preparations for invasion. He stayed at Boulogne for about a year, waiting his chance. On this side of the Channel, counter preparations were made for the defence of Kentish soil. Martello towers were built; military forces were assembled; canals were dug; defences were made; large numbers of volunteers – the forerunners of our present Local Defence Force – were raised and armed; and – no invasion took place!

Similarly, during the last War, very complete arrangements were made to face the threat of invasion, both in the south-eastern counties and in East Anglia. That will be in the memory of many of you. Again – no invasion took place.

Now, once more, we have before us the possibility of invasion, and already extensive military preparations are being made, as many of you have seen – to meet a possibility which cannot be ruled out – and these are very wise precautions; and the Government would be greatly to blame if such precautions were not taken.

As the War has developed, especially recently, it is quite clear that the civil population becomes more and more drawn into the battle area. So much so, that if there were invasion, it would have a very definite and very vital part to play. People are, naturally, asking what that part is; and very briefly I would like to-night to state what is the duty of the citizen – the average citizen, man or woman – if unfortunately the threat of invasion should materialise.

Let us assume the worst just for the sake of argument. And first of all let us consider the question from the German point of view. What is it that the German would like to see as the result of his setting foot, whether from the sea or from the air (or from both) on these shores? I will tell you. He would like to see what he has seen in Poland, in Norway, in Holland, and in Belgium. He would like to see an immense amount of confusion. He would like to know that rumour and despondency spread, and spread quickly. He would like to see the roads thronged with a procession of hapless refugees on foot and in vehicles, because this would have two effects; firstly, it would give admirable and unresisting targets for his airmen; and secondly, it would tend further to spread chaos and distress, by the bombing and the machine-gunning of the defenceless fugitives. And above all, he would particularly like to see the crowds of fugitives blocking the roads and preventing the advance of our troops to deal with his attack.

Now the answer to all this is quite obvious; and it is the civilian who has got to give that answer. In the first place, everybody, especially those holding public positions, should be alert. And in the second place, every citizen must be determined that he will <u>not</u> spread rumour: that he will <u>not</u> block the roads; that he will <u>not</u> become a fugitive; that he will, in fact, keep his head clear and his mouth shut, and that he will "stay put" and sit tight; because, firstly that is the best way to help our own soldiers and airmen; and secondly, it is for his own protection that he or she will be far safer in his or her house, than on the roads.

So, there are the golden rules if ever we are taken by surprise. First; sit tight. And secondly, do not move on any orders except such as are delivered to you by a responsible official.

Now in particular – I would like to address myself, if I may, to two classes of people who are extremely important; firstly to those men and women of influence and authority in any community; the people of prominence, who can do an immense amount of good by their personal example. And secondly, to those upon whom depend the life of the community and the prosecution of the War; and by that I mean the municipal officials, the civil defence workers, the heads and staffs of large industrial and commercial establishments; the Post Office officials and the telephone workers; everybody who is engaged in the work of public utilities; the doctors, and the ministers of religion, and so on.

Well, I'm afraid this is rather a gloomy subject; but these are stern times, and it seems to me that everything is to be gained by being frank, and everything is to be lost by being unprepared. We have had, as you know, previous threats of invasions; and those threats have not materialised. There is no reason why it should not utterly fail. And fail it will, if everyone will keep his head and do his duty. And here the civilian has just as important a national duty to carry out – difficult as it may seem – as the sailor, the soldier, or the airman.

I have just two more words to say. Some people, who are in a position to do so, are now moving from the coast inland; and there is no reason why they should not – provided always they are not any of the individuals to whom I have just referred. Those must stay. Indeed it may be that for military reasons (that is to say, to help the soldiers) the Government will take steps later on to evacuate from certain places, portions of the civilian population as a precautionary measure, just as we have evacuated some of the school children. If such Government action is to take place, ample warning will be given, and it will be the duty of those concerned to co-operate. Rest assured that clear and precise instructions will be issued about this, so that every man and woman will know in time what to do about it. And in the meantime – Carry right on!

TUESDAY Home Service

BLACK-OUT STARTS—

London 7.0	Plymouth 7.18
Cardiff 7.12	Leeds 7.2
Edinburgh 7.5	Aberdeen 6.57

A.M.

7.0 Time, Big Ben : NEWS
and summary of today's programmes
for the Forces

7.15 MORNING STAR
Records of Dick Todd, 'the
Canadian Bing Crosby'

7.30 UP IN THE MORNING
EARLY
Exercises for men : Coleman Smith
7.40 Exercises for women : May
Brown

7.50 'TUNE FOR TODAY'
An anthology of favourites

7.55 LIFT UP YOUR HEARTS !
Short morning prayer

8.0 Time, Greenwich : NEWS
Programme Parade

8.15 THE KITCHEN FRONT
Mrs. Buggins (Mabel Constanduros,
Recording)

8.20 'LET US BE GAY'
Gramophone records

9.0 REGINALD KING
with his Quartet

Moorland Fiddlers .... Arthur Wood
Interlude for Sentiment Leslie Bridgewater
Irish Tune .... Aberdeen
Allen Blue Gown .... Barratt
Rural Life in Bohemia .... Fletcher
Julia : Windflowers .... Reginald King
Scherzo .... Tchaikovsky

8.35 'ESSAYS IN ADVENTURE'
12—Cyril Gardiner

This well-known actor began his career by
going out to Australia as a 'jackeroo'.
Today he tells the story of an eventful
career, taking his from the Australian
back-blocks to stage and film work in
many parts of the world.

8.45 JAMES BELL
at the theatre organ

Trumpet Voluntary .... Jeremiah Clarke
Lovers' Waltz .... (wrongly ascribed to Purcell)
Fair House of Joy .... Quilter
Intermezzo for Little Folk : 'In the Wood'
Cry of Little Bo-Peep .... Rex Harty
On a Welsh Air : David of the White
Rock .... arr. Edward German
Hark ! the zephyrs are turning .... Kreisler
Waltz : Eugene Onegin .... Tchaikovsky
American Patrol .... F. Tschudi

10.5 FOR THE SCHOOLS
News commentary and interlude

10.15 Time, Greenwich
THE DAILY SERVICE
from p. 17 of 'New Every Morning'
and p. 12 of 'Each Returning Day'

10.30 'CLOSE HARMONY'
Record programme of famous trio
and quartet singers

10.45 'WISE HOUSEKEEPING'
'What's wrong with English house-
keeping ?' Views from Poland,
France, and Holland

11.0 FOR THE SCHOOLS
11.0 PHYSICAL TRAINING (for use in
halls or playgrounds) : by Edith
Dowling.
11.20 Interval music
11.25 GAMES WITH WORDS :
arranged by Helen F. Benson
11.40 TALKS FOR FIFTH FORMS :
Electricity in the service of man.
'Electricity for Everyman' : C. W.
Harson .

P.M.

12.0 BBC
SCOTTISH ORCHESTRA
Conductor, Guy Warrack
Overture : Libella .... Reisiger
Two fantastic Melodies for strings
.... Coates
Airs de ballet (Lalo) .... Grundman-
Overture in a Comedy .... Balfour-Gardiner

12.30 'WORKERS' PLAYTIME'
Lunch-time entertainment for factory-workers, from a factory somewhere in Britain

1.0 Time, Greenwich : NEWS

1.15 AMERICAN COMMENTARY
Recording of last Saturday's broadcast by Elmer Davis

1.30 HANDEL
Arias, sung by Stiles-Allen with the
BBC Northern Orchestra, conducted
by Leslie Howard
Wilt the sun forget to streak ! (Solomon)
Arioso : Load on star (Joshua)
Angels ever bright and fair (Theodora)
With thee the unsheltered moor I'd tread
(Solomon)

1.50 FOR THE SCHOOLS
1.50 FOR RURAL SCHOOLS : Country
work and country ways. 'Good
Seed ': visit to a seedsman who is
'out for quality '.
2.10 Interval music
2.15 FOR UNDER-SEVENS : Let's join
'm. The story of the clever little
red hen
2.30 Interval music
2.35 SENIOR ENGLISH II : Good
writing. Dramatic biography : W.
H. Davies, by S. P. B. Mais. Story
of W. H. Davies's life illustrated by
extracts from 'Autobiography of a
Super Tramp', and his poems

3.0 MUSIC WHILE YOU WORK
Rhythmic records

3.30 EVENSONG
from a college chapel
Versicles and Responses
Psalm 119, vv. 1-16
First Lesson : Proverbs 4, vv. 10-18
Magnificat (Byrd : Second Service)
Second Lesson : St. Luke 15, vv. 1-8
Nunc Dimittis (Byrd : Second
Service)
Creed and Collects
Anthem : Bow thine ear (Byrd)
Prayers
Lord, when we bend before thy
throne (E.H. 79)

4.0 NORRIS STANLEY
and his Sextet, with Ronald Bristol
(tenor)
SEXTET
Selection : Waltzes from Vienna
.... Johann Strauss
RONALD BRISTOL
So we'll go no more a-roving .... White
SEXTET
Dairy Lady .... Wright
Summer Breeze .... King
RONALD BRISTOL
Shine through my dreams .... Novello
Sylvia .... Speaks
SEXTET
Serenade .... Schubert
Novelty : Pantaloon .... Curzon
RONALD BRISTOL
Kishmul's Galley .... arr. Kennedy-Fraser
My heart, the bird of the wilderness
.... Mallinson
Trav"in' to the Fair .... arr. Sandford
SEXTET
Jensen Polka .... Browne
Hornpipe (Pronto with modern)... Ross
Poem : a West Country ball

4.45 'THE STATUE'
Short story written for broadcasting
by H. Baerlein, and read by G. R.
Schjelderup

5.0 Newyddion (News in Welsh)

5.5 AWR Y PLANT
(Welsh Children's Hour.) 'Y Clor
Cyntaf'. Drama-flantasi i blant gan
E. Eynon Evans, wedi ei chyfieithu
gan Eic Davies

5.30 CHILDREN'S HOUR
5.30 Nursery programme, devised
for very small children by David
5.45 'Lessons from famous Soccer
matches', by P. N. S. Creek. No. 2.
'Internationals'

6.0 Time, Greenwich : NEWS
National and Regional announcements

6.30 News in Norwegian

6.45 'CAN I HELP YOU ?'
Weekly series of talks to help
listeners to carry out smoothly the
many regulations which are so important for the war effort on the home
front

7.0 'SALUTE TO LATIN-
AMERICA'
BBC Orchestra. Conductor, Sir
Adrian Boult. Tom Bromley (piano)
ORCHESTRA
Overture : Il Guarany .... Carlos Gomes
Sospiranda Poem : El Cisne (The Swan)
Tito .... O. Q. Bianco Lafuta
TOM BROMLEY AND ORCHESTRA
Fantasy for piano and orchestra
.... Alfonso Leng
ORCHESTRA
Batuque (Negro Dance) from Brazilian
Suite .... Oscar Lorenzo Fernandez
See 'Radio Music' on page 4

7.45 'FEARAS-CHUIDEACHD
HAM BARD'
Orain, sgeulachdan-eile is feala-dha,
le Iain A. MacNeacail 'na fhear an
tighe. (Gaelic light programme)

8.15 THE (WELSH) BRAINS
TRUST
answering 'Any Questions ?' More
than 500 Welsh listeners have sent in
question for the Welsh edition of the

H. W. NEVINSON,
one of the greatest of war corre-
spondents, and a crusader in many
causes, died at the end of last year
aged eighty-five. A tribute to the
man and his work will be broadcast
tonight at 10.35.

Brains Trust and some of the best
will be answered by Sir Wynn
Wheldon, Professor W. J. Gruffydd,
Emlyn Williams, Professor-Emeritus and
Canon and Canon Maurice Campbell, with a Scots
Question-Master, Donald McCul-
lough, and a Welsh producer,
Howard Thomas. (Specially recorded
to be repeated next Sunday in the
Forces programme at 4.0)

9.0 Time, Big Ben : NEWS

9.25 TONIGHT'S TALK

9.40 MELODIES FROM THE
COMEDIES
Sung by Violet Carson and Dennis
Noble, and played by the BBC
Theatre Orchestra, with Donald Edge
at the piano. Compère, Pat Curwen.
Programme arranged and conducted
by Reginald Burston

10.20 'LIGHTEN OUR
DARKNESS'
Evening prayers

10.35 'I KNEW NEVINSON'
Tribute to a modern knight-errant,
the late Henry Wood Nevinson—
journalist, crusader, scholar, and
rebel—with an introduction by his
artist son, C. R. W. Nevinson. By
Cyril Ray and Erik Dunroue. Produced by Robert Kemp

11.5 VIOLIN SOLOS
played by Michael Zacharewitsch
Adagio in E .... Mozart
J. Beautiful .... Mozart
La Source d'Arethuse .... Szymanowski
A la Zingara .... Wieniawski

11.25 OSCAR RABIN
and his Band

12.0 midnight-12.20 a.m.
Time, Greenwich : NEWS

TUESDAY for the Forces

342.1 m. 877 kc/s. 48.86 m. 6.14 Mc/s

A.M.

6.30 GREETINGS
to the Imperial and Allied Forces in Great Britain (recording), followed by

' NEVEILLE !'
Cheerful gramophone records

7.0 Time, Big Ben : NEWS
Programme summary

7.15 MORNING STAR
Records of Dick Todd, ' the Canadian Bing Crosby '

7.30 THESE WERE NEW...
three years ago
Popular records of February 1939

8.0 Time, Greenwich : NEWS
Programme Parade

8.15 ' LET US BE GAY '
Gramophone records

9.0 REGINALD KING
and his Quartet
(for Home Service)

9.35 JACK BENNY PROGRAMME—1
Repeat of the special recording broadcast on Sunday

10.0 ' ACCENT ON RHYTHM '
Recording of Sunday's broadcast

10.15 ' SUT HWYL ?'
Darnau difyr ar y bore, sef, penatil, ac ronglen a chan, gyda'r ambell arni ddigrif. Y flaglen dan odd John Griffiths. (Welsh light programme)

10.30 MUSIC WHILE YOU WORK
Louis Voss and his Orchestra

PAUL BEARD,
leader of the BBC Symphony Orchestra, talks about his work in the new series ' The Orchestra Speaks ', today at 1.15.

11.0 Time, Big Ben
ERIC SPRUCE
at the theatre organ
March of the Bowmen...............Curzon
Marigold.............................Mayerl
Selection : Sunny......................Kern

11.15 BBC
MIDLAND LIGHT ORCHESTRA
Conducting, Richard Crean
March : Hampton Court..............Graham
Overture : The Merrymakers, Eric Coates
Waltz : Wine, Women, and Song...Strauss
Selection : The Student Prince...Romberg

11.45 ' KING PINS OF COMEDY '
No. 78—Charlie Kemble. The Interviewer, Richard North

P.M.

12.0 PLANTATION SONGS
BBC Men's Chorus, conductor, Leslie Woodgate; Joseph Farrington (bass), at the piano, John Wills
Some folks like to sigh.......Stephen Foster
Old 'Cabin Home; be early in the morning ; Kingdom coming
......................................Scottish S.S.R.
Nelly Bly.......................Stephen Foster
Billie Blue.....................Scottish S.S.R.
I shall I'm sorrow ; Come where my love lies dreaming ; The Glendy Burk
...............................Stephen Foster
Click ! Clack ! Scott Getty, arr. Woodgate
De Ole Banjo....................arr. Woodgate

12.30 ' WORKERS' PLAYTIME '
Lunch-time entertainment for factory-workers, from a factory somewhere in Britain

1.0 Time, Greenwich : NEWS

1.15 ' THE ORCHESTRA SPEAKS '
2—The leader. Presented with gramophone records by Paul Beard, leader of the BBC Symphony Orchestra

1.35 OSCAR RABIN
and his Band
Oscar Rabin's Band, this week's ' dance band of the week ', is famous for many things—its number of its popular singers, Diane and Beryl Davis ; and the comprising by Beryl's father, Harry Davis. Oscar Rabin himself is one of the very self-effacing band-leaders before the public. On stage engagements he plays less and saxophone and sits in with the band. It was the BBC band-leader to have his special triumph. Many members have been with the band for many, many years for the whole sixteen years of its existence.

Time, Greenwich, at 2.0

2.20 OLD WELSH BALLADS
(Hen. Falell). Ceinwen Rowlands (soprano), Trefor Jones (tenor), the Welsh Light Orchestra, conducted by Idris Lewis. Programme devised by Sam Jones and Idris Lewis
This programme includes old Welsh ballads popular in fairs and market places in Wales during the last century. Some of them, such as ' Y Mochyn Du ' (The Black Pig) and ' Y Ferch o Rederyn ' (The Maid of Pendeyn) have an unusual history.

2.45 SANDY MACPHERSON
at the theatre organ

3.0 MUSIC WHILE YOU WORK
Rhythmic records

3.30 BBC VARIETY ORCHESTRA
Conductor, Charles Shadwell, with Frank Tinterton, in a concert of light music

**4.15 ' SINCERELY YOURS—
VERA LYNN '**
Special recording of the Sunday evening ' letter from home to the Forces ', with Vera Lynn and Fred Hartley and his Music

4.45 ' THESE YOU HAVE LOVED '—31
Doris Arnold brings you some more gramophone records of ' classic ' songs and melodies that you know and love

Time, Greenwich, at 5.0

5.30 ' THE WORLD AT WAR '
Questions on current affairs from men and women in the Forces answered at the microphone by Vernon Bartlett

5.45 JOHN HILTON TALKING

6.0 Time, Greenwich : NEWS
National and Regional announcements

6.30 ' JUST JUDY '
with Judy Shirley, Dick Francis, and Dorothy Summers. Script by Henrik Ege. Ivor Dennis at the piano. Produced by Eric Fawcett

6.45 ' FOR THE AVERAGE PLAYER '
Expert advice on popular games: Snooker ; first of three ' refresher ' lessons by Joe Davis, World Champion 1927-1941
(See the article on page 3)

7.0 NEW ZEALAND NEWS-LETTER
Jack McGuire presents the week's news from home for New Zealanders in this country

7.5 AUSTRALIAN NEWS-LETTER
Weekly summary of Australian news specially prepared for Australians in this country, and read by George Ivan Smith

7.15 ' MAKE AND MEND '—10
Magazine programme devised by Peter Creswell, and presented by him, to, for, about (and largely by personnel of) the Royal Navy. Produced by Peter Creswell and Peter Watts
Esmond Knight spins a yarn
H.M.S. ' Incredible ' ship's concert
Mrs. Wilson's weekly letter from her son, Stoker (1st Class) ' Tug ' Wilson
' Leave it to the Navy '—being the adventures of two simple sailors, by David Yates Mason. Episode 2
' This week's new number ': Harry Bidgood's Band and Chorus, in original tunes by Signalman Geoffrey Wright and others
' The Briny Trust ' : Cadet Rating J. B. G. Thomas, Leading Writer Roland Blackburn, and Petty Officer

JOE DAVIS
gives more hints for the ' Average Player ' in three broadcasts, starting this evening at 6.45.

Writer Robert Burgess attempt to reply to ' What's the buzz ? '
Music editors, Signalman Geoffrey Wright and Harry Bidgood. General editor, Paymaster Sub-Lieutenant David Yates Mason, R.N.V.R.

8.0 ' RECORD TIME '
with Roy Rich

8.30 JACK PAYNE
with his Orchestra

9.0 Time, Big Ben : NEWS

9.25 CYRIL FLETCHER
in ' Odes and Ends '. Special recording of the ninth of a weekly series with Betty Astell, Frederick Burtwell, and the Dance Orchestra, conducted by Billy Ternent. Script by Dick Pepper. Produced by Ronald Waldman

9.55 GREETINGS
to the Imperial and Allied Forces in Great Britain (recording), followed by
' MURRAM FOR HOLLYWOOD !'
' Guts, guns, and gangsters '. Another smartmoth million-dollar epic from the Dreamtone Studios. Hollywood burlesque, with records, devised and written by Roy Plomley and produced by Frederick Piffard. Cast includes Dorothy Carless, Alan Keith

Time, Greenwich, at 10.0

10.25 LEONARD
and his Orchestra with Rosa Lewin and Peter Valerio
Antiga mia (My Friend)........Muriatia
Emerald Express..................Chevron
What happens When we........Sarosh
Waltz : Acceleration..............Strauss
You're in my arms....................Carr
Some Chicken ! Some Neck !....Forsyth
Caprice Jongrois................Victoria
A Dream of Hawaii...............Hartley
Red Moon Over Havana..........Firman
A Midsummer Night's Dream....Thomas
Selection : Idler Trio...Schubert—Clutsam

11.5 Close down

BRITAIN AT BAY
G.P.O. Film Unit

Commentator

For nearly a thousand years these fields and farmsteads of Britain have been free from foreign invasion. We've not known even a civil war for close on 200 years. We have been a fortunate people.

But not all of us live in such peaceful solitude . . . Our great wealth has come from our industrial towns. Though these towns are anything but perfect dwelling places, though we've long been anxious to improve them – have improved them – they are ours, and all we ask is to be left alone to do what we like with our own . . . And never far away from even the blackest town is the most beautiful countryside in the world . . . Till there suddenly came upon us the menace of war. It came because Nazi Germany was determined to flourish, not by peaceful trading with her neighbours, but by ruthless aggression and conquest. Its vast military machine was created at the expense of all the decencies and amenities of civilised life. It was set in motion. It swallows up Czechoslovakia. It invaded Poland. It invaded Norway. Without warning it over-ran Holland and Belgium. It invaded France, driving millions of refugees in front of it as if they were cattle. Using every vile and treacherous stratagem it compelled the Bordeaux Government to ask for an armistice. This has left Britain alone – at bay.

It's not the first time that she's been at bay against a concrete tyranny, for we were equally alone against the full might of Napoleon, who ruled an area greater than Hitler rules now.

The future of the whole civilised world rests on the defence of Britain. First, of course, on the Navy . . . and the army . . . and the Air Force . . . and then on all of us. Britain must become impregnable citadel of free people. These people of ours – as easy-going and good natured as any folk in the world – who asked for nothing belonging to others but only for fair dealing among nations – I say, these people – our people – are now hurrying to man this island fortress. All the war industries are speeding up – speeding up. Millions are toiling day and night at a pace never equalled in our history.

A great many devoted citizens used the first long weary months to train themselves for such a moment as this. The time has now arrived when their numbers must be greatly increased. There are many essential services, calling now for recruits. We need nurses, stretcher bearers, firemen, Civil Defence workers. Or, again, we can begin our own military training. Here are some factory workers who have organised their own defence force. All over the country our homes are now being guarded by the ground watchman – the Local Defence Volunteers, and we know already that their eyes are keen, and they are prompt to take action. They're our reply to the German parachute troops. Another reply equally valuable is just sticking to our jobs when we know that these jobs are important. But those who can fight will fight, and alongside us are men from our great dominions – Australia, New Zealand and Canada. In the new famous words of our undaunted Prime Minister – "We shall fight on the beaches, we shall fight on the landing grounds, in the fields, in the streets. We shall fight in the hills. We shall go on fighting, breaking their black hearts, until all nations now imprisoned can come out into the sunlight again. Till all good men everywhere are free."

THE END

List of Shots

M.L.S.	Waves breaking on sea shore
L.S.	Fields
L.S.	"
L.S.	Sheaves of wheat being collected
L.S.	" " "
L.S.	" " "
L.S.	" " "
M.L.S.	People closing locks
L.S.	Factory from canal
L.S.	Town
M.C.U.	Chimney pots
M.L.S.	Building with scaffolding round it

L.S.	Street from one end
L.S.	Town train passing in foreground
L.S.	Town
L.S.	Cattle on hillside
L.S.	Sun setting behind hill
M.L.S.	Bomb exploding
C.U.	Thick black smoke
M.C.U.	German troops marching past
C.U.	Same shot but from behind Hitler
C.U.	German troops marching past
C.U.	Hitler
C.U.	German saluting from passing tank
L.S.	Aerial shot of troops marching past
M.L.S.	Do.215 taking off
M.C.U.	Germans closing barrier
M.L.S.	Two Germans guarding street. Pan to crowd of people
L.S.	Burning shores of Norway
M.C.U.	He.111 in flight
V.L.S.	Aerial shot of town from plane
V.L.S.	" " "
M.L.S.	Bushes and Barn
M.L.S.	He.111 in flight
M.L.S.	Blitzed town
M.L.S.	French refugees walking along road
M.C.U.	French refugees
C.U.	French refugees on cart
C.U.	French soldiers firing rifles
M.L.S.	French soldiers in battle
C.U.	Man writing notice
L.S.	Cliffs of Dover
M.L.S.	" "
C.U.	Waves breaking on shore
L.S.	Map of England
C.U.	Waves breaking
M.L.S.	Waves breaking over rocks

C.U.	Keel cutting through water
L.S.	Formation of Cruisers
M.L.S.	Soldiers on motor bikes
M.L.S.	Ansons in flight
M.L.S.	Man with sacks
M.U.C.	Large gun
L.S.	Big Ben
M.C.U.	Men looking at notice
M.C.U.	Men running to join in rank
L.S.	Men marching
M.C.U. to C.U.	Men marching towards Camera
M.C.U.	Foundry workers
M.C.U.	Women operating machines in factory
M.C.U.	Men foundry workers
M.C.U.	Steam Flames
C.U.	Foundry
C.U.	Woman working machine
M.L.S.	Foundry worker
M.C.U.	Series of factory interiors about [illegible] long
L.S.	Fire station
L.S.	Firemen using hoses
L.S.	Firemen using hoses on burning building
L.S.	Ditto
C.U.	Notice
C.U.	"
C.U.	"
M.C.U.	Nurses nursing patient
M.L.S.	Stretcher bearers going in building
M.C.U.	Fireman sliding down pole
M.C.U.	Two firemen holding nozzle of hose
M.C.U.	Canteen workers
M.L.S.	Men marching (L.D.V)
C.U.	Men marching (L.D.V)
L.S.	L.D.V. in training
C.U.	L.D.V. marching

C.U.	L.D.V. man presenting arms
M.L.S.	L.D.V. on parade
M.L.S.	L.D.V. marching through wood
M.C.U.	L.D.V. on top of building
M.L.S.	Church tower
L.S.	Aerial view of street
L.S.	Aerial view of men in fields
M.C.U.	Men pulling swedes
M.C.U.	Telephone operator
M.C.U.	Practising with a bayonet
L.S.	Destroyer of "Jervis" class and the "Empress of Britain"
M.L.S.	"Empress of Britain"
M.C.U.	Australian soldiers marching past
M.C.U.	Scottish soldier
M.C.U.	Mr. Churchill in car
C.U.	Soldier on guard on beach
M.L.S.6	Crew and "bofors"
L.S.	Soldiers advancing and lying down
M.L.S.	Soldiers by street barrier
M.C.U.	Soldiers manning field gun
L.S.	Soldiers on hills
C.U.	End of barrel of gun
M.L.S.	Tanks coming towards camera
L.S.	Landscape

"Britain at Bay."

1. A compilation of Library Material, with some new shooting, based on an idea conceived by J.B. Priestley and made by the G.P.O. Film Unit within seven days.

New Shooting:- (with War Office facilities).

Shots 1–3, 16, 17, 41, 45, 50, 55–58, 71–73, 79–86, 98–103.

Library Material:-

(i) G.P.O. Films, including: "Spring Offensive"; "Voice of Britain"; "Forty Million People"; "Men in Danger"; "Cableship"; "Horney Hall"; "Factory Front"; "ss Ionian"; "Able Seamen"; Cinemagazine

(ii) British Newsreels: Movietone; Paramount; G.B. News.
(iii) Canadian material; War Office. Both unspecified.
(iv) French Material: "May, 1940"; Journal de Guerre.
(v) Captured German Material: "Baptism of Fire"; Newsreels.
(vi) "Jamaica Inn"; "Convoy". Both Feature Films.

2. <u>Scripting, financial authorities, etc.</u>:-
Scripting by J.B. Priestley, who also generally assisted in the construction of the film, for a fee of £50. (See Minute dated 13/7/40 on G.P.O. file F.2387).

G.P.O. Film Unit authorised to produce the film at a maximum length of 800ft., the cost not to exceed £1 per foot direct charges. (See our letter dated 20/6/40 on file F.149/52/11 and Minute dated 26/6/40 on G.P.O. file F.2387).

Finance authorised £2.2.0d to cover fee of cameraman Allen White. (See authority dated 23/6/40 on G.P.O. file F.238).

Finance authorised £3.3.0d to cover fee of cameraman James Rogers. (See authority dated 23/6/40 on G.P.O. file F.2387).

3. <u>Music</u>:- Specially composed for the film by Richard Addinsell for a fee of 15 gns.

Directed by Muir Mathieson for a fee of 10 gns.

4. <u>Commentary</u>:- Written and spoken by J.B. Priestley.

5. <u>Distributions</u>:- Theatrical in 5 Minute Series.

6. <u>Foreign Versions</u>:- The film was re-titled for foreign distribution, "BRITAIN ON GUARD."

CHAPTER 6

WORK

ON YOUR WAY TO THE NEW JOB
*The Chief Inspector of Factories
sends you this message*

If you are going to work in a factory for the first time, I hope you will read this on your journey or before going to the new job. Even if you are now changing over from a small factory to a large munition works, you may get some help from these short notes.

The first week in a large works is very like the first week in a new school. You will be in strange surroundings and will find yourself among a busy set of people, all of whose work has to be carefully arranged in order that the finished article may be turned out quickly and well. Your first friends will be your FELLOW WORKERS. If approached in the right way, you will find them willing to help and show you the ropes. They will help you to learn your way about and give you useful tips on your own particular job, on what to do and what to avoid; do not be afraid to ask them. You will soon discover the friends who are most willing to help.

Your next friends will be your CHARGEHAND AND FOREMAN OR FOREWOMAN. These are very busy people but you will find they are ready to help you with the details of your work and they are not of the severe type that was common in my young days. Next to a good workman, a foreman loves a good time-keeper. Remember the foreman has a kind of jig-saw puzzle to complete each week and *your* absence will upset that puzzle, so avoid unnecessary risks of injury or ill-health. In this connection, may I advise you to think of the importance of your own particular piece of work, even if it is the making of one small part over and over again. Your pieces are designed to fit into the whole; they may be parts of a machine gun, an aeroplane or even a battleship and unless your pieces are forthcoming, the whole is held up. I think we can all get the greatest help in thinking about the ultimate results of our own efforts to help the country.

If you are going to a large works, you will probably find there a Personnel or Labour Department, including a WELFARE OFFICER. In fact, your first contact will probably be with that Department, whose officers are there to help you, and you should not hesitate to get into touch with them on any question of difficulty.

In a large works you will also probably find a WORKS DOCTOR and QUALIFIED NURSES in charge of an ambulance room. The doctor will be ready to help you on questions of your health, though he may advise you to go to your panel doctor for further advice and treatment. The nurses are available to attend to minor ailments and, in particular, to injuries. Do not neglect minor cuts and scratches. They can easily become infected and lead to blood poisoning, and the only way to avoid this is to get immediate first-aid attention. I have known death result from a prick from a wire because the wound was allowed to get infected. Proper first-aid attention will make these little accidents the trivial things they appear to be. In my time, if one got anything in one's eye, there was always a pal who was prepared to take it out with the end of a matchstick. We know better now. Your eyes are too valuable to trust to unskilled treatment, so do not let anyone touch your eyes except someone skilled in first aid.

Large works usually have a FACTORY CANTEEN and I hope you will soon find your way to it. A good meal a day is important for a hard worker, and if your home life is upset by night air raids, etc., you may also find it possible to use the canteen for breakfast and tea. If the food shortage gets worse, you may not always find in the canteen the food to which you are accustomed, but this subject has been carefully studied and you should find there the food that is available, served up in appetising and most nourishing ways.

In these war days you may be asked to work longer hours than in peace time. It will help you to do so if you take advantage of the rest pauses for a real rest and for some refreshment either from the canteen or from trollies.

You should also make yourself acquainted with the AIR RAID SHELTERS and any means of local protection that is provided in the shop. The means of escape that you are expected to use in case of fire should also be known to everybody. Fire fighting and A.R.P. equipment is meant for use in sudden emergencies. Do your part by getting to know what is expected of you and keep all the equipment and passage ways clear of obstructions.

If you are put to work a MACHINE, be sure you know your job and do not interfere with it while it is running. Machines are very obedient things, but they will usually only stop when someone makes them stop, so be sure in the first place that you know how to do this. While they are running, the parts that cut metal or wood will also cut fingers. If things go wrong, stop the machine and see the chargehand or foreman. Do not interfere with guards provided for certain parts of your machine. They are put there because, in the opinion of experienced people, they are necessary for your protection. It is not because you are thought to be careless but because experience has shown that we cannot think of everything at once. When we are intent on our work, we may, without knowing it, place our limbs in danger. These guards and other precautions such as goggles, etc., may seem a nuisance at first, but if you learn to use them from the beginning, you will soon be so accustomed to them that they will not interfere with your work. Your clothing also will help. Women are well advised to avoid high heels and to keep their hair under a cap. Loose sleeves and neck ties will be picked up like lightning on a revolving tool and may take you with them. A good close-fitting overall is an undoubted precaution and looks workmanlike. A good worker is always a safe worker. Your work is valuable and Mr. Bevin has said that "every accident is a bonus to the enemy," because in your case it deprives the country of your services.

Most of the accidents in factories, however, are not due to machines but to little things that can only be avoided by care. Watch an old skilled craftsman and you will see that he has a place for every tool and his work is orderly and neat. Try to imitate him. Good housekeeping is as valuable in a factory as in the home, both for your protection and for speed of work. Look out for nails, sharp corners, ends of wire; littered floors mean broken knees and defective hand tools mean injuries sooner or later.

I am sending you this message because it is my job to look after safety, health and welfare in factories, and Factory Inspectors (whose nearest address you will find on the Abstract of the Factories Act posted up in the works—usually near the entrance) will always be glad to give you further advice on these subjects. If you cannot find the address of the local Inspector, your Trade Union representative will know it, or you can write to me direct.

You are going among a crowd of the best-hearted people in the country, full of humour and just inclined to pull your leg at first, but also full of commonsense and proud of the value of their work. I hope you will be happy as one of our great industrial army helping to win this war.

A. W. Garnett
H. M. Chief Inspector of Factories
Ministry of Labour and National Service

WELCOME THE WAR WORKER

Keep this Leaflet
It Answers Your Questions

Message From the Minister of Labour and National Service

TO THE HOUSEHOLDER

I ask your support, as head of the household, in my appeal to the housewives of the nation.

With THEIR help and YOUR co-operation the job can be done.

What is the job? Plainly and simply to win the war and to win it quickly.

To win the war our Navy, Army and Air Force need ships and more ships, tanks and more tanks, aeroplanes and more aeroplanes.

To produce them, more and more war workers must be employed in our shipyards and factories.

In your district, more living accommodation is needed for these workers.

I appeal to you to give a welcome to war workers as lodgers in your home.

Make them comfortable and you will increase their efficiency.

That will be a contribution YOU can make towards winning the war.

And remember, it is a vital contribution

Ernest Bevin

You are asked by the Government to Welcome War Workers as Lodgers

In doing this you will help to make more workers' services available to the war effort and will thus be performing a very important piece of war service.

You have perhaps never taken a lodger before and you may feel it a bother to have a stranger in the house, but in these times when everything is at stake, personal convenience must yield to the needs of the country.

Here are the Answers to Frequent Questions

Why not build houses or hutments?

Because building labour and building materials are so urgently needed for building factories, aerodromes and defence works and repairing damaged houses that they cannot be spared. Also, building takes time and the war effort demands the utmost speed in production.

How do I get a war worker as a lodger?

You may receive a visit from a Billeting Officer, or a representative of a voluntary organisation whom the Billeting Officer has asked to help him.

The Billeting Officer seeks in the first place your voluntary co-operation in offering lodging accommodation on agreed terms.

If you have a spare room in your home and have not heard what to do to get a lodger, write to the Billeting Officer at the Town Hall, or go to see him.

Can I be compelled to take a lodger?

The Government have power to compel householders to provide accommodation to war workers.

In some places where there is a shortage of accommodation offered voluntarily, Billeting Officers are already authorised to use these powers.

If you receive a Billeting Order you cannot refuse to take the worker billeted on you. If you wish to appeal against the Order you may do so, but until your appeal is heard by the appropriate Tribunal you must obey it.

How About Washing and Baths?

The lodger will need to have access to water for washing and if you have a bath in the house you will find it a good thing to agree on fixed times for the various people in the house to have the use of the bath.

If you have no bath, tell the lodger where the public baths are.

Do I provide meals for the lodger?

If you are able to provide meals, the lodger will usually wish to make an arrangement with you to let him have his breakfast and a hot meal in the evening; his mid-day meal he will probably get in the factory. If he is on night shift he will probably still wish to have two meals in the house. On Sundays, if he is not working, he will probably in most cases like to have three meals.

But whether you volunteer to take a lodger or have one billeted on you, you are not obliged, in any circumstances, to provide meals. It may not be possible for you to provide them; you may be out at work all day yourself.

If you cannot provide any meals for the lodger, explain this to the Billeting Officer when he comes to see you.

What kind of meals will be needed?

You will probably be able to arrange with the lodger, without much difficulty, what is to be given to him to eat. People's likes and dislikes vary, and if he comes from another part of the country he may want dishes you cannot give him. But perhaps you can give him things to eat he will like even better.

Men and women working long hours require meals suited to their needs. There are various ways in which help and hints may be obtained in providing such meals in wartime. For instance, information about food and many useful recipes are given at 8.15 a.m. every day on the Home Service of the B.B.C. Further, "Food Facts" advertisements appear every week in newspapers all over the country telling what foods to buy and different ways of using them.

Demonstrations of cooking, specially suited to war-time conditions, are given in many towns and useful leaflets are distributed.

It is worth while consulting the food chart in the Ration Book. It helps you to plan your meals by choosing foods from the three main groups, protective, body building and energy foods. The chart shows all the alternatives in each group so that if one food is not available, another of the right kind can take its place.

What else can I do for the comfort of my lodger?

Try to make your house a "home from home" for your lodger. He will appreciate anything you are able to do for his comfort. For example, he may like a quiet corner for reading or writing.

If he works on night shift, make as little noise as possible about the house when he is sleeping. Don't turn on the wireless too loud.

If his clothes are wet when he comes in in the evening, let him hang them to dry in the kitchen or some warm place.

If you have time to do any darning or mending for him, he will be grateful.

Such attention to his comfort will be appreciated, and he on his side will probably be only too glad to do things about the house in his spare time.

If your lodger is a woman she will like to have hot water sometimes to do some of her washing.

How will I be paid?

If you volunteer to take a lodger you will arrange directly with him what he is to pay you for board and lodging, or for lodging only if you are unable to provide meals.

If your lodger is compulsorily billeted on you, you will receive a form which will entitle you to be paid by the Post Office 5/- a week for each lodger to cover the cost of his lodging. If you voluntarily provide board as well, you will arrange directly with him what he will pay for board.

What should I do if my lodger falls sick?

If your lodger falls sick, send for the District Nurse. She will know what to do.

If he is likely to be in bed for some time and you cannot look after him, the doctor will probably be able to arrange for him to be moved to one of the emergency hospitals which have been set up by the Ministry of Health.

What must I do if my lodger leaves?

If your lodger leaves, whatever the reason may be, it is very important that you should let the Billeting Officer know at once.

GOING AWAY ON WAR WORK
Keep This Leaflet
You Will Find It Useful

Message From the Minister of Labour & National Service

In these days, I have to ask a great many workpeople to take up jobs away from home; we are all in this war, and have a part to play in the struggle against the common enemy whether we are in the fighting services, in the factory or on the building site. I realise that for many such a move is quite a new experience, and the purpose of this leaflet is to provide the answer to some of the questions you will want to ask. If there is anything more you want to know, or if you are in any difficulty, remember that the Employment Exchange is there to do all they can to help. I wish you all success in your new job.

Ernest Bevin

If you are being transferred by the Ministry of Labour and National Service to war work there are probably a number of questions which you want to ask. Here are the answers to some of them:—

What must I take with me?

You must remember to take your Identity Card, Ration Book, (which you should ensure has all its pages and is in order), Unemployment Book, National Health Insurance Card, Medical Card, Gas Mask, Membership card of any organisation you belong to, Post Office Savings Bank book.

Don't forget about change of underclothing, spare socks and stockings, a second pair of boots or shoes and washing things, as well as your working clothes, boots and tools. As towels are now on coupons you must take your own towels with you. Take some food for the journey and a cup. You may not get tea unless you have your own cup, as these are scarce in station buffets. Make sure that your luggage is labelled with the coloured labels the Employment Exchange will give you.

What about fare, travelling time and lodging allowances?

Your Employment Exchange will tell you and give you a leaflet about these allowances.

If you are in any difficulty about providing for your needs on the journey explain the position to the Exchange, who may be able to help you.

What about the journey?

The Employment Exchange in your home town will, if necessary, give you information about the journey, particularly the train to catch and where to change. Check up with the station staff on the journey but do not ask other passengers for advice; they are almost sure to be wrong, and as a result you will arrive at the wrong place or at the wrong time and so upset the arrangements made for you at the other end.

What shall I do when I get to the station at the other end?

You will probably be met by someone who will know you are coming and will give you the help and directions you need.

It may be impossible to arrange for anyone to meet you, or your train may be late and so upset the arrangements which have been made. Your home Exchange will probably have given you an address to go to; if they have not done so go to the nearest Exchange when you arrive. If it is night time, the Exchange will be closed. Go to the Station Master's Office, show him this leaflet and ask him for advice.

Will lodgings be found for me?

The Employment Exchange will help you to find lodgings. Being away is not quite the same as living at home. Your landlady may not always understand exactly what you like. Also she may not be used to having anyone in the house, any more than you are used to being away from home.

Give and take must be on both sides.

What about meals?

Your landlady may be able to provide your meals but when it is not possible for her to do so (she may herself be doing war work) you should find out whether there is a canteen in your factory or whether one of the British Restaurants has been set up in your district. There may be a club near by which provides meals. You can get advice from the Citizens' Advice Bureau.

What happens if I am ill?

If you need nursing ask your landlady to call in the district nurse. She will always be willing to help and you will only be expected to contribute what you can afford. If you cannot be looked after in your lodgings your doctor can arrange for you to be looked after in one of the Emergency Hospitals which have been got ready by the Ministry of Health. You can go there even if you are not ill enough to think of going to hospital in the ordinary way. Make use of these services at once and don't wait till you are really bad.

Put your name down at once with a panel doctor as soon as you arrive in the new town. There is a list of panel doctors at the Exchange.

Give to the Personnel Supervisor or Welfare Officer at the factory and the local Employment Exchange the name and address of your mother or other near relative. Tell your landlady or the Warden of your Hostel, too, just in case it is necessary for them to get in touch. The Exchange will make special arrangements for a near relative to come and see you if you are seriously ill.

If you subscribe at home to friendly societies, doctors' clubs and other organisations to cover yourself or your family for medical and nursing attention, you must see that you remain in benefit even though you are away. See your secretary or collector before you go and arrange for your family to continue to pay contributions, or, if you belong to a national society, ask him to transfer your membership to the lodge or branch in the town to which you are going. If there is a sick club in your new job, join it. It will save you a lot of anxiety.

What can I do with my spare time?

The people in the place you are going to have clubs and social centres very like your own and you will be welcomed there. Where there are a lot of workers going into a place, new societies and clubs are started and you will be able to join with others who like the same sort of entertainment and hobbies as you do. If you belong to any organisation at home which has branches over the country get the address of the new branch before you leave home. Ask at the Exchange or the Citizens' Advice Bureau if you want to know what society you can join and what the local amusements are. They can advise you and they may be able to give you a leaflet showing particulars of local clubs and other activities in the district.

Who deals with complaints?

The local Exchange can always help you even if your difficulty has to go to someone else in the end. Call there and get advice. The Minister of Labour and National Service has appointed a Welfare Officer in each place where there are a lot of new factories and it is his job to help men and women engaged on war work to feel at home in the new towns. The Welfare Officer can be reached through the local Employment Exchange. Don't throw up the job just because you feel strange at first. Remember your work is helping to win the war.

TRAFFIC—QUEUES
STATUTORY RULES AND ORDERS 1942 NO. 517
EMERGENCY POWERS (DEFENCE)
THE REGULATION OF TRAFFIC (FORMATION OF QUEUES) ORDER, 1942, DATED MARCH 16, 1942 MADE BY THE MINISTER OF WAR TRANSPORT.

The Minister of War Transport, by virtue of his powers under Regulation 70 of the Defence (General) Regulations, 1939, and of all other powers enabling him in that behalf hereby orders as follows:—

1. Where at any stopping-place (including a stand or terminus) on a tramcar, trolley-vehicle or public service vehicle route on any highway provision is made, by means of a barrier rail, or of two parallel barrier rails, for the formation of a queue or line of persons waiting to enter the vehicle such persons shall form and keep the queue or line in manner following that is to say:—

The queue or line shall commence against the end of the barrier rail or parallel barrier rails nearest to the stopping place of the vehicle and facing the said stopping place and shall continue alongside the barrier rail, or (in the case of parallel barrier rails) between the barrier rails.

2. Where no barrier rail is provided, any six or more persons so waiting as aforesaid shall form and keep a queue or line of not more than two abreast on the footway.

3. A person shall not take or endeavour to take any position in a queue or line formed in accordance with the provisions of paragraph 1 or paragraph 2 of this Order otherwise than behind the persons already forming the same, or enter or endeavour to enter the vehicle before any other person desiring to enter the same vehicle who stood in front of him in such queue or line.

4. This Order shall come into force on the 12th day of April, 1942, and may be cited as "The Regulation of Traffic (Formation of Queues) Order, 1942."

Signed by Order of the Minister of War Transport this 16th day of March, 1942.

G. F. Stedman.

CHAPTER 7
INVASION

STAY WHERE YOU ARE
Issued by the Ministry of Information on behalf of the
War Office and the Ministry of Home Security

If this island is invaded by sea or air everyone who is not under orders must stay where he or she is. This is not simply advice: it is an order from the Government, and you must obey it just as soldiers obey their orders. Your order is "Stay Put", **but remember that this does not apply until invasion comes.**

Why must I stay put?
Because in France, Holland and Belgium, the Germans were helped by the people who took flight before them. Great crowds of refugees blocked all roads. The soldiers who could have defended them could not get at the enemy. The enemy used the refugees as a human shield. These refugees were got out on to the roads by rumour and false orders. Do not be caught out in this way. Do not take any notice of any story telling what the enemy has done or where he is. Do not take orders except from the Military, the Police, the Home Guard (L.D.V.) and the A.R.P. authorities or wardens.

What will happen to me if I don't stay put?
If you do not stay put you will stand a very good chance of being killed. The enemy may machine-gun you from the air in order to increase panic, or you may run into enemy forces which have landed behind you. An official German message was captured in Belgium which ran:

"Watch for civilian refugees on the road. Harass them as much as possible."

Our soldiers will be hurrying to drive back the invader and will not be able to stop and help you. On the contrary, they will have to turn *you* off the roads so that they can get to the enemy. You will not have reached safety and you will have done just what the enemy wanted you to do.

How shall I prepare to stay put?

Make ready your air-raid shelter; if you have no shelter prepare one. Advice can be obtained from your local Air Raid Warden or in "Your Home as an Air-raid Shelter", the Government booklet which tells you how to prepare a shelter in your house that will be strong enough to protect you against stray shots and falling metal. If you can have a trench ready in your garden or field, so much the better, especially if you live where there is likely to be danger from shell-fire.

How can I help?

You can help by setting a good example to others. Civilians who try to join in the fight are more likely to get in the way than to help. The defeat of an enemy attack is the task of the armed forces which include the Home Guard, so if you wish to fight enrol in the Home Guard. If there is no vacancy for you at the moment register your name for enrolment and you will be called upon as soon as the Army is ready to employ you. For those who cannot join there are many ways in which the Military and Home Guard may need your help in their preparations. Find out what you can do to help in any local defence work that is going on, and be ready to turn your hand to anything if asked by the Military or Home Guard to do so.

If you are responsible for the safety of a factory or some other important building, get in touch with the nearest military authority. You will then be told how your defence should fit in with the military organisation and plans.

What shall I do if the Invader comes my way?

If fighting by organised forces is going on in your district and you have no special duties elsewhere, go to your shelter and stay there till the battle is past. Do not attempt to join in the fight. Behave as if an air-raid were going on. The enemy will seldom turn aside to attack separate houses.

But if small parties are going about threatening persons and property in an area not under enemy control and come your way, you have the right of every man and woman to do what you can to protect yourself, your family and your home.

Stay put.

It's easy to say. When the time comes it may be hard to do. But you have got to do it; and in doing it you will be fighting Britain's battle as bravely as a soldier.

INDEX